D0458394

What a Difference a Dog Makes

ALSO BY DANA JENNINGS

NONFICTION

Sing Me Back Home

FICTION

Lonesome Standard Time

Women of Granite

Mosquito Games

CHILDREN'S

Me, Dad & Number 6

What a Difference a Dog Makes

Big Lessons on Life, Love, and Healing from a Small Pooch

DANA JENNINGS

Doubleday
New York London Toronto
Sydney Auckland

DOUBLEDAY

www.doubleday.com

DOUBLEDAY and the DD colophon are registered trademarks
of Random House, Inc.

Frontispiece photograph by Deborah Feingold

LIBRARY OF CONGRESS CATALOGING-IN-PUBLICATION DATA
Jennings, Dana Andrew.
What a diffference a dog makes : big lessons on life, love, and
healing from a small pooch / by Dana Jennings. — 1st ed.
p. cm.
1. Jennings, Dana Andrew. 2. Prostate—Cancer—
Patients—New Jersey—Biography. 3. Miniature
poodle—New Jersey—Anecdotes. 4. Human-animal
relationships—Anecdotes. I. Title.
RC280.P7J46 2010
362.196'994630092—dc22
[B]
2010018632

ISBN 978-0-385-53283-9

PRINTED IN THE UNITED STATES OF AMERICA

1 3 5 7 9 10 8 6 4 2

First Edition

For my wife, Deborah—

forever and ever, amen

Author's Note:
Bijou de Minuit,
Canine Zen Master

In their mysterious and muttish ways, our dogs become our teachers. When I think about Bijou, I realize that besides being the family dog, she has also been a life coach—an accidental Zen master, if you will.

If you pay close attention to your dog's behavior, there are any number of simple and useful lessons to be learned—proving that it isn't necessary to spend thousands of dollars and burn a month at some rarefied mountain retreat to find true enlightenment.

Some dogs are Seeing Eye dogs, but Bijou has opened our eyes and she has become our Seeing Life dog.

She has, for example, taught us:

Nap in the sun whenever possible.

Play, even when you're old and creaky.

And live in the moment: Eat when you're hungry. Drink when you're dry. And be sure to attach yourself to a visitor's leg when the spirit moves you. (Yes, Bijou is a female, but she's a *dominant* female.)

These are just a few of the lessons from Bijou that we have taken to heart—well, except for the part about the visitor's leg.

But rather than squander all of her wisdom in a single chapter, I have seeded Bijou's nuggets to live by throughout this book, between chapters. And if you want to skip ahead and read them first—like tasty doggie treats—go right ahead.

I myself have one more teaching to go with Bijou's. The dust-encrusted cliché tells us to stop and smell the roses. But I say: Stop and pet the dog. I always make sure I give Bijou a friendly rub before I head out the door in the morning.

What a Difference a Dog Makes

Introduction: Miracles in the Moment

Our dogs constantly surprise us. They are our four-legged verbs: They dance when we come home from work, they fetch when we fling the ball, and they come running and panting when we call their names. Dogs are miracles in the moment—they teach us, in fact, that each moment is an absolute miracle—and they live in the eternal present. They don't fret over past mistakes, or dwell on past glories, either. The future is always now.

We invite our dogs into our lives as "just the family pet," but often they end up being canine candles that blaze and shine, illuminating our lives. My family's furry candle is a miniature poodle named Bijou de Minuit (Jewel of Midnight), and over the years she has taught us countless lessons about life, love, and healing.

Besides being the family dog—the only role we ever expected of her—Bijou has been a drinking buddy and a fuzzy shrink, an alarm clock and an angel of mercy, a sleeping partner and a sun worshipper, bunny-lunger and carcass-snuffler, beggar-dog and thief, ear-sniffer and tail-chaser, and, in the end, a devoted mystery with a cold black nose.

When my younger son, Owen, and I were both seriously ill—him with liver failure, me with an aggressive prostate cancer—Bijou became even more than verb and miracle. She was a healing presence in our lives. Believe me, when your life is reduced to a large question mark, nothing feels better than having a twenty-three-pound mutt snuggled up next to you. Owen and I both profoundly understand what a difference a dog makes.

The summer that I recovered from radical surgery, Bijou would jump onto my sickbed, nuzzle me, and ask for her ears and pointy snout to be scritched and scratched. It made both of us happy as she sighed in doggish satisfaction.

As I lazed and dozed at home, there was nothing sweeter in the world than to hear Bijou drink from her water dish outside my door, the gentle sound of her measured lap-lapping ferrying me to waters of healing.

And she was the subject of one of our favorite family jokes during my recuperation:

"You take the dog out. I have cancer."

I spent a lot of time spading the past that summer. And fittingly, my very first memory is of a dog:

It's dawn and I'm standing in my crib. Dad is holding up

a wriggling puppy and it's licking my face—possibly administering my first baptism by tongue—and making me laugh.

That's it, as sharp and fleeting as a dream.

I asked my parents about that memory, wanted to confirm the truth of it, and they told me that the dog was a black Lab puppy. A few weeks after we got her, she bolted out of the house and onto Route 125, where she was hit and killed. My folks couldn't recall her name.

A poor unknown puppy—oh, let's call her Midnight—undone by her doggish exuberance over fifty years ago. And yet, she still lives in my memory, squirming and yipping and licking . . . and the thought of her too short life makes me want to cry, just as most thoughts of Bijou make me smile.

Bijou is ordinary in being extraordinary. Good dogs—and most dogs are good dogs, if given a chance—grant us the grace of their brief lives.

The ancient rabbinic sages believed that in saving one life it was as if the entire world had been saved. In that spirit, I would argue that in writing about one dog it is as if I am writing about the entire world, writing about every dog that has ever blessed our lives.

Here is the story of the one dog that I know best—my Every Dog—Bijou de Minuit.

Possession
Or, the Curious Incident of the Dead Bird in the Kitchen

Like James Brown, that late, great Godfather of Soul, dogs love the funk.

Given a choice between a gentle stroll through a dandelion-dappled field and a romp and roll through the muck and the mire, a dog will go for the mud bath every time—the more foul and oozy the better. Sometimes, I think, dogs believe that they are actually four-wheel-drive vehicles with fur and tails.

Dogs are connoisseurs of crunchy rabbit droppings and rank roast beef, of skanky, sweat-soaked socks and underwear, and the chance to give a deep snuff-snuffle to a dead possum, skunk, or woodchuck is heaven on earth.

Bijou is no exception. She might have that snooty little poodle pedigree, but her instincts are all mutt. And given that they're all nose, dogs have a clear advantage over us humans when it comes to detecting that delectable world of reek and skank.

So, it's a quiet Sunday morning, my two boys are still asleep, as boys often are, my wife, Deb, is rustling in the kitchen, and Bijou and I are shuffling toward the back door. I hook her to the leash, but when I open the door she pauses—"Come on, Bijou"—sniffs, then lurches at what looks like a small pile of leaves riffling on the deck.

When she dashes back into the house instead of rushing down the walk to relieve herself, I—being a shrewd dog owner—know that something's up.

"What've you got in your mouth, Bijou?" I hear Deb say.

"Grrr."

"Bijou?"

"Grrr."

"Oh, *gross!* Dana, she's got a bird! She's got a bird!"

At least it's dead . . . I hope.

Bijou retreats to the far corner of the kitchen, the bird still planted in her mouth, its wings and feathers sticking out from either side of her lathered jaws.

"Oh, cool, Bijou's caught a bird!"

"It was dead," I say.

Our sons, Drew and Owen, who are always pumped for a confrontation between Dad and dog, have stumbled and rumbled downstairs. Whenever Mom shrieks "Oh, *gross!*" that's a hard-and-fast signal to jump out of bed and scamper downstairs.

And, of course, there's nothing quite like the spectacle of watching Dad and Bijou go mano a doggo.

"Whatcha gonna do, Dad?" the boys ask, their eyes gleaming with glee. It's like having Animal Planet right there in the kitchen—except I'm no unflappable crocodile hunter.

I try the straightforward dog-master approach first (knowing full well that it won't work). I stride over to Bijou, look her in the eye, and firmly say: "Bijou. Drop it."

"Grrr."

All right, so we raised our kids better than we raised our dog. One more time: "Bijou. Drop it."

"Grrr."

No question, Bijou's brain has been short-circuited by bird lust. What she really wants to do is carry her prey off to some dark, feral cave, eviscerate it, and chow down on the choicest bits. Instead, she's cornered—how embarrassing—in a kitchen in suburban New Jersey. That never, ever happened to Cujo.

Deb tries next, still hopeful. "Bijou, want a treat?" She shakes the box of Milk-Bones at her like some kind of Native American shaman—talk about desperate housewives.

Bijou gives her a baleful glance: "Yeah, right."

I crouch in front of Bijou and slowly reach toward her—"Beeee-jouuuu, drooooop iiit"—and somehow simultaneously her jaws tighten on the bird (mercifully, it *is* dead) and her lips curl back in a snarl. To be honest, I don't like how she's glaring at my bared throat.

Bijou: "Grrr."

Deb: "*Dana, be careful.*"

Bijou: "Grrr."

Boys: "She gonna bitecha, Dad?"

Bijou: "Grrr."

Me: "Boys, get me the gardening gloves."

Bijou: "Grrr."

Well, poodle wrestling isn't anywhere near as glamorous as alligator wrestling, but sometimes it just has to be done. And, of course, in my family I'm the designated poodle wrestler (not to mention poodle wrangler).

The boys secure their spots on the kitchen bleachers as I tug on my garden gauntlets and become Sir Dana the Mortified of Godfrey Road, unhorsed, if not unmanned, by a minipoo. I swear that my sons are gorging on popcorn and Jujubes as they watch, but I'm probably mistaken.

I march over to Bijou—"*Dana, be careful*"—bend over her, and try diplomacy one last time: "Bijou. Drop it."

"Grrr."

I reach down and start prising open Bijou's jaws with all the pride of a sneak thief pinching candy from a baby.

"Grrr."

It's really, really amazing how hard a miniature poodle can keep her jaws clamped shut.

"Grrr," and "*Dana, be careful*," and "You're getting there, Dad."

I feel like Johnny Weissmuller in one of those old Tarzan movies where he kills the crocodile or lion by artfully avoiding the rows and rows of dagger teeth and wedging open the animal's jaws to the breaking point.

I don't want to hurt Bijou, of course. I just want to get that *goddamned bird* out of her mouth.

Firm yet gentle, I unlock Bijou's jaw—the poodle giving me the wolf eye—and unmesh her teeth. When I manage a gap in Bijou's mouth, I shout, "Now, Drew!" and he swipes the dead bird away, Deb expertly sweeps it out the door, and Bijou detonates into a one-dog riot.

She snakes her lip back to her forehead, bares her cute little white fangs, snaps a couple times so that her teeth clack and click, then dervishes around the kitchen, chasing her tail—Little Miss Psycho Poodle. It's all quite charming.

We let her cool off, then, fifteen minutes later, I call to her. "Bijou, let's go out."

I hear her head shake as if she's waking from a dream, she trots down the stairs, I hook her up, and we take our walk—all is forgiven, with no hard feelings on either side.

Bijou de Minuit,

CANINE ZEN MASTER, SAYS:

When you feel threatened, throw a bad look and growl. It usually works. If it doesn't, run like hell and cower behind your owner.

Squealin' Pigs 'n' Leapin' Lizards: Starter Pets

Dogs don't arrive in our lives in a vacuum.

Like many parents, Deb and I tried out a range of starter pets on Drew and Owen when they were little boys before granting them the gift of a dog: guinea pigs and Russian dwarf hamsters, a clutch of lizards and penny goldfish.

(The goldfish, "won" at school fairs, always used to weird me out. Whenever I looked at them, treading water in their tiny bowls, they always seemed to be saying: "Why me? Why me? Why me?" This led me to one of my rules for leading the good life: Accept no pets that can be brought home in a plastic sandwich bag. Even a goldfish can teach a lesson.)

Without quite realizing it, we had turned our house into a manic menagerie of squealing (and randy) guinea pigs, leapin' (literally) lizards, and furtive hamsters. I did have to keep reminding the boys, though, that the field mice that liked to conga through our cellar in winter in search of warmth, crumbs, and hot apple cider didn't qualify as true pets.

Here are a few field notes.

Guinea Pigs Are Easy, Too Easy

Let's face it, guinea pigs are appallingly cute. While in the wild they might be most any predator's hors d'oeuvre of choice—no carnivore's dilemma there—in a mall pet shop they push that primal button that makes us go: "*Ooohhh.*"

Meanwhile, the emerald green viper a couple cages down is sticking its skinny red tongue out at us because it intuitively knows that we're a bunch of naïve idiots.

Anyway, it seems as if we accelerated from owning two guinea pigs to being overrun by thirteen of the dainty varmints in about a week.

The pet store clerk, of course, had assured us that both of our guinea pigs were female. Apparently, though guinea pigs are notoriously hard to sex, they have no trouble at all having sex. It could also be that pet store clerks are just innately evil.

Before we knew it, we were guinea pig farmers: "Time to get up, boys. We've got to milk the pigs," or something like that. Our third-floor hall had become a suburban barnyard of four or five cages, bales of alfalfa, and sacks of chow. You know how some people give away their late-summer bounty of tomatoes and zucchini? We were giving away guinea pigs.

I was the one who slopped the wee hogs each morning. And the moment that my hand turned the doorknob to the third floor, the squeals started—"*reent-reent-reent*"—each and every one of those pigs sounding—"*reent-reent-reent*"—as if they were being skinned and dismembered—"*reent-reent-reent*"—instead of just hungry.

Yeah, no shortage of guinea pigs. There was Butterscotch and Pepper, Oreo and Brownie, Cinnamon and Nutmeg. I felt like Miss Jean on the old *Romper Room* TV show, greeting the eager kids out in TV Land each morning.

The first time one of the boys shouted, "The guinea pig's having babies!" we all trundled upstairs, ready to play rodent midwife. By the fifth or sixth time, we'd just call back, "Uh-huh, just let us know when she's done."

But when the piglets started being born with extra toes, we realized that enough was enough.

There's no underestimating guinea pig lust, however. After we had separated the adult pigs, trying to halt the population explosion on the third floor, I watched one day as Brownie, flexing his little piggy knees, jumped and somehow managed to scramble up the cage wall like an army ranger and tumble into the adjacent cage, where his true love waited all a-tremble.

Brownie got scooped up, dropped back into his bachelor pad, and mesh covers were put in place. Guinea pigs also squeal—"*reent-reent-reent*"—when they're hungry for love.

Save for their talent to reproduce, guinea pigs *are* good starter pets. They purr. They like to nestle and nuzzle. And if you watch them long enough, you're bound to see one execute the Guinea Pig 180. This happens when the pig gets startled and leaps, managing to get four feet off the ground and spin its plump, pear-like carcass 180 degrees.

So, yeah, guinea pigs *are* really, really cute. But if you're not interested in the art of animal husbandry, only bring one home from the pet store.

Lizards Are Hard, Too Hard

When my oldest son, Drew, was a kid, he wanted lizards.

Lizards were cool (literally). Lizards were poker-faced. Lizards were like small, cold-blooded skateboards. That's how cool they were.

This was, of course, well before the brown-and-white tiger lizard—we didn't quite know what it was, we just called it a tiger lizard—vaulted from Deb's cupped hand to the top of Drew's head, where it triumphantly kneaded his hair as if preparing to make a nest.

"Get it off! Get it off!"

Obviously insulted, the tiger lizard long-jumped off Drew's skull and proceeded to dart, bound, and cartwheel around the room until exhausting itself. I didn't realize until that moment that lizards could pant. The pet-store clerk, of course, had assured us that tiger lizards were as docile as great-grandma on Valium and simply *lived* to have their scaly hides stroked.

Back we went to the lizard store, our ex-pet skittering in a shoebox. After steering Drew away from the snake department—I'm the kind of guy who has a recurring nightmare of Hydra-like serpents writhing on the light fixture above our bed—we arrived home with a couple of smallish green and generic (we thought) lizards. In fact, we called them the Generics.

"They're going to stay in their cage, right, Dad?"

"That's right, Drew."

"We're not going to take them out, right?"

"No, Drew."

"And they can't escape, right?"

"Nope," I said, but with slightly less conviction.

God, lizards are stupid. They fry themselves on the heat rock—"Ooohhh, that feels really good, Manny. Hey, wait a minute! My scales have melted!"—they let dinner (crickets) hike on their backs, and they eat each other. You'd think they were running for public office in New Jersey.

The lizards didn't do much for me. They'd mope around the cage. I'd stare at them. They'd stare at me. To be honest, the crickets had more personality.

Then came the day when we were witness to one of the true mysteries of nature.

A quiet, rainy afternoon, the boys playing upstairs. I'm

reading a Stephen King novel . . . "Daaaad! The lizard's having babies!"

"What?"

"The lizard's having babies!"

"Are you sure?"

"Oh, no! The dad just ate its tail!"

I sighed, set my book down, and trudged upstairs. Lizards don't have babies, I thought, they lay eggs. They're *reptiles*, fer cryin' out loud, and reptiles lay eggs.

The lizard was having babies.

Right there, in the cage, as Drew, Owen, the father lizard, and I watched. Two or three newborns were already flitting and scooting about the cage, including the one whose tail had been bitten off by the old man. We immediately named him Stumpy.

With the mom still in labor—it's true, it isn't easy being green—we plopped our new reptilian additions into their own terrarium, and flicked the dad away as mom finished up. As Owen said later, "It was like National Geographic, right there in Drew's room."

The pet store clerk, of course, had assured us . . . oh, just to hell with it.

As I've said, lizards are hard. Baby lizards are even harder. Without the warmth of the heat rock, they die. But if they bask too long, they sizzle. Because they were so small, we had to feed them tiny, tiny crickets—crickets so minuscule that they figured out how to sneak out of the terrarium, with the baby lizards not too far behind.

I got home one night at two in the morning, peeked into Owen's room, where we kept the babies, and saw that all four of them had creeped from the terrarium and were clinging to Owen's dresser all in a line, like a scaly freight train.

Lizards, man.

Despite our best efforts, all of the lizards died, with Stumpy hanging on until last, taking his final toasty rest on the heat rock.

The crickets, on the other hand, thrived. Months and months later, we'd open a dresser drawer or a closet door and hear the faint *chirp-chirp* of a cricket, reminding us all of the day that the lizard had babies.

Bijou de Minuit,

CANINE ZEN MASTER, SAYS:

If you need to bark and howl, bark and howl. Dogs don't keep their feelings buried inside. Thus, they rarely take Zoloft or Prozac.

Something Wild

One of the most profound lessons that cancer taught me was how to slow down—how to defy our modern lives pared and splintered into microseconds, how to savor each singular moment. That was a lesson also reinforced by Bijou in her resolute dogginess.

And in my slowing down, I studied Bijou, my accidental Zen master, even more closely.

When I stare into Bijou's brown eyes, for all her easy domesticity, I still see a residual wildness that stirs there. So it doesn't shock me too much when she sometimes stands on point in the backyard, one paw tastefully raised, her snout lifted into the night breeze and sifting the air as if she were some canine wizard in search of signs and portents. (I have to admit, though, that watching a miniature poodle—that consummate house dog—stand on point never fails to make me smile.)

Bijou will occasionally howl, too, which gives all of us the willies but makes us laugh, too. I'll never forget the first time she let loose with a howl—a deep and genuine "*ow-ow-owooooo!*"

She had stationed herself at the top of the stairs, her warm-weather command post at the confluence of all the upstairs cross breezes, to drowse. Then Owen began practicing on his recorder, low and mournful and, apparently, utterly dog-worthy.

Bijou bolted awake, sat up, and belted out an aria of howls that would've done any wolf or coyote proud: "*Ow-ow-owoooo! Ow-ow-ow-owoooo!*"

Owen stopped playing: "Dad, did you hear that!"

With Owen no longer yowling on the recorder, Bijou stopped howling. She took her bows, then slumped back to her nap, as if saying: "Yeah, I know how to do that. Pretty cool, huh? You oughta hear me wail on the tenor sax, baby."

Yeah, wild.

Even when she licks my feet, her bubblegum tongue slipping and sliding between my toes, I don't feel that she's doing me any favors. I'm simply her very convenient salty snack—not quite as good as sour cream and onion potato chips, but good enough—the same as if she and her wolf cousins had found a handy salt lick out in the primeval woods.

Then there's Bijou's daily dance with the neighborhood bunnies. In fact, that could be her Native American name, Dances with Bunnies.

Because we lack natural predators, except for the occasional oblivious SUV, our block is overrun by a plague of rabbits. In high summer, they lounge in the shade of the hedges and play checkers, peer insolently from their hidey-holes and brazenly graze—*nibble*, *nibble*, *nibble*—on our lawns. And they drive Bijou crazy.

When Bijou and I head down the back steps for a walk, there are almost always a couple of rabbits dallying in the backyard. When they hear the door shut, their noses flare, they get that nervous, Don Knotts look in their wide and wary eyes and become very, very still: "If I don't move, they won't see me . . . If I don't move they won't see me."

But Bijou isn't fooled. She shrugs off her chic suburban airs and circles her prey, urging me on with just a subtle tug of the leash. And given that I'm now packing a fully loaded poodle, a small voice sputters in my head that sounds suspiciously like Elmer Fudd: "*Be vewy, vewy quiet, I'm hunting wabbits. Heh, heh, heh.*"

As Bijou skulks toward the bunnies, she gets lower and lower and *lower* as the rabbits get stiller and stiller and *stiller*. Bijou creeps . . . they take a couple steps sideways; Bijou skulks . . . they shuffle. And then she leaps, lunging at the bunnies and making them scatter and hightail in a cloud of downy cotton butts.

Jerked back by her leash, Bijou scowls at me for my ungentlemanly *rabbitus interruptus* and gives me the requisite evil wolf eye—"Gee, thanks for all the help, Dad"—and stalks off to find a patch of grass to water.

So, yes, I divine wildness in Bijou's eyes. But, too, when I stare into the mirror at my own blue-green eyes, I can still see a glint of wildness there, too, a comforting youthful wildness that still smolders and that most people don't suspect. But it's that mutual wildness in man and dog that, I believe, led us to choose each other.

Because that's one of the big mysteries, right? How did we choose dogs, and how did they choose us?

What do we see when we stare into each other's eyes? What deep mammal bond lurks there? Why do we stoop for a strange dog and ask to scratch its soft, irresistible ears? And why does that same dog give us the hard lean against our legs that tells us, "Hey, man, you're all right."

Oh, I know that the biologists and the anthropologists think they have answers to those questions. But their dry science isn't satisfying, doesn't roll around in the mud and revel in the mystery of it all.

There's something essential in the physical transactions between human and dog. When Bijou jumps onto the couch, circles a couple times, then plumps herself down next to me and sighs in contentment, that act sums up why we bring dogs into our lives: We savor the beauty of the fact that the miracles of their lives so comfortably intersect with the miracles of our own.

Bijou de Minuit,

CANINE ZEN MASTER, SAYS:

When the sun rises, it's time to get up.

(If, however, it's pouring, curl into an even

tighter dog ball—and hold it.)

Bijou, Angel of Mercy

Bijou has no overwhelming desire to please, which is part of her regal charm.

Maybe it's because we live in New Jersey, but whenever I ask Bijou to do something—"Hey, Bijou, bring me a dram of Glenfiddich. Neat"—I often get the "What's in it for me?" look.

"You want me to snuggle next to you on the couch? Then fork over part of that roast beef sandwich, pal—hold the pickle." Or, "You want me to fetch? That'll be at least ten minutes of ear-scratching."

You know, the ol' you wash my paw and I'll lick yours quid pro quo.

She's much more interested in pretending to be twenty-three pounds of furry fury, though she drops that pose with Deb.

She knows the sound of Deb's Volkswagen Passat and has

built an elaborate ritual around discerning the thrum of that magic motor.

When Bijou hears the car, her head snaps to and she squeals that squeal of canine joy that almost sounds like murder. Then, no matter where she's resting, she sprints to Drew's room, vaults onto his bed, and peers out of the window that overlooks the driveway—her tail jitterbugging.

When Deb steps foot out of the Passat, Bijou shrieks and yelps then scampers down the stairs, slips on the hardwood landing as she bangs a left into the kitchen and waits, barely contained and almost levitating, at the back door.

Once Deb opens the door—squeal! squeal! squeal!—Bijou's dancing on her hind legs, front paws paddling the air, throwing wet kisses, and sticking her cold black nose in Deb's ears.

When I come home, unless she has to go out, I get the lazy, lizard-like glance (and, here, I thought I was done with that)—"Oh, it's you. Don't forget to wipe your feet this time"—before she resumes her VIN: Very Important Nap.

So, no, Bijou isn't quite what you'd call a classic therapy dog. In fact, she seems a more likely candidate to receive therapy than to deliver it. Even so, the summer of my cancer surgery, she was a crucial part of my recovery.

It seemed as if she understood that I'd been reduced to a kind of animal vulnerability. She'd leap up on my sickbed and snug her small curl of sleep into my larger curl. Or she'd give my feet a couple ticklish licks and then settle at the foot of the bed, as if guarding me. Sometimes, she'd find just the right spot next to the bed, do her little circle waltz, emit her soft sigh of descent, then flop on the floor, granting me the gift of her nearness.

Her simple presence brought me pleasure. Whenever she strolled into the room it was as if she were giving me a transfusion of her doggish energy.

Other times, she would just stand quietly next to the bed and I'd reach down and scritch-scratch her head and ears, working my fingers into her fur and body, seeking her very essence, the healing powers of dog flesh.

My younger son, Owen, and I share a lot of things. We're both smitten with Seamus Heaney's translation of *Beowulf*, we were both high school runners, and Johnny Cash's end-of-the-road rendition of the song "Hurt" devastates us each time we hear it.

But Owen, who is twenty as I write this, and I also share a deeper and darker knowledge than what usually passes between fathers and their sons in their youth.

As I've said, I had prostate cancer. And when Owen was a senior in high school, his liver failed, suddenly and for no apparent reason. He has since recovered, but when we look at each other these days, we are still bound and pierced by our mutual sense of mortality.

Young men expect their fathers to live forever. And fathers never expect to outlive their sons. But Owen and I profoundly understand that there are no sure bets in this life.

Those first days when Owen's liver failed were the absolute worst of my life. My wife and I met with a liver transplant team, and intimations of death hung unspoken in the air. To watch your critically ill son sleep fitfully in his hospital bed is nearly unbearable. But you do it, because not to watch is even worse.

In just a few days our soccer-playing, 200-meter-sprinting son became exhausted and sore and turned yellow (including the whites of his eyes). A high school senior less than ten days from prom and graduation, Owen was admitted to New York–Presbyterian Hospital on May 31, 2007—patient no. 3743472. He was in liver failure, diagnosed definitively as type II autoimmune liver disease only after he was discharged and all the test results were in. His immune system had turned on his liver. His body was in revolt.

The hospital's pediatric liver team shocked his system with staggering amounts of steroids and pumped him full of fresh frozen plasma to try to stabilize him. After six days he was released, weak, tired, and still faintly yellow, as if he'd been brushed with pollen. He made his prom, though, long enough to get his picture taken—his high school girlfriend, Kate, brilliant and beautiful in a bright yellow dress—and got to graduate with his classmates.

It wasn't the first time that Owen had had biological bad luck. In 2005, both of his lungs had to be surgically repaired when, four months apart, each one spontaneously collapsed. That was difficult for our family, but nowhere near as intense and grueling as when his liver failed.

The lung operations were a mechanical problem, in a sense like fixing a couple of flat tires. But his liver failure was systemic.

And Bijou, the dog that he had pined for when he was just eight years old, provided unexpected solace during Owen's illnesses that none of us could have foreseen.

"When I was fifteen and my lungs were collapsing," Owen wrote after he had recovered from his liver failure, "it was like Bijou was always there, wagging her tail, licking me, barking incessantly, tap-dancing on the landing outside my bedroom.

"Taking as many pills as I do to control my immune system can be daunting. But it's always comforting to know that Bijou is taking just as many for her ailments. If she's taking that many, then I can do it, too—right? She was kind of like a mascot when I was really, really sick, encouraging me toward health and going through the same stuff that I was going through.

"Because of Bijou, a part of me came to understand my illness was just a natural part of my life. There didn't have to be a reason for getting sick. If Bijou was getting sick, our little harmless innocent poodle, then clearly there was no omnipotent creator punishing me. I was just sick. She was just sick. People and animals get sick—that's just how life works.

"Seeing Bijou have an intense epileptic seizure in July of 2007 probably meant more to me than it did to the rest of our family. I saw her lying there, convulsing, drooling, helpless. There was no way to make her feel better. We just had to wait.

"I understood this better than anyone. No matter how much I wanted to get better, my body just needed time. I was like Bijou. We would both be OK, eventually, but we just needed to be patient, give our bodies time to heal."

And not that it's necessary—or even helpful—to lay genetic blame, but there's a good chance that it was my genes that led to Owen's autoimmune liver disease. There's no guilt or finger-pointing here, just simple DNA-based evidence.

In early 1982, when I was twenty-four years old, I learned that I had ulcerative colitis, a disease in which the immune system attacks the colon for no good reason. By the fall of 1984, the disease was so fierce that I spent six weeks in the hospital and needed twenty-seven units of blood. My colon had to be surgically removed, so I've had no colitis since. The only reminder is the plastic pouch I wear on my abdomen.

Owen and I don't overtalk our bond, our respective situations. When you share knowledge at the cellular level, sometimes there isn't much to say. We do talk, of course, but often it's enough to just sit in the den and take in an international soccer game or listen to Mr. Cash croak and gasp through "Hurt," with Bijou tucked right between us.

No matter what's happening in your life—even if your son is lying in the hospital, critically ill—the dog still needs to go out, still has to be fed, still needs to get *her* pills. But that's not a bad thing.

Contrary to what people who resist dogs think, dogs don't disrupt our lives, but bring normality to them. In most any family, it's the dog who is full of common sense. She knows when she has to pee, knows when she wants a treat. When it's hot and humid, she holes up in the room where the AC is. When it's arctic and snowy, she hugs the kitchen radiator.

Dogs don't piss and moan about what's happening at work, don't start shouting matches over math homework or beg to borrow the car, don't fret and obsess over their 401ks. Normal. The poet and mystic Rumi said, "Become the light." Dogs are light.

We'd get home late when Owen was in the hospital, but I was too wound up to go to bed. Each night, I retreated into the den with a Harpoon ale, put on a CD—*Kind of Blue* by Miles Davis, anything by the forlorn British folk singer Sandy Denny—and sat in the dark with my even darker thoughts.

After a few minutes Bijou would follow me in, her nails click-clicking on the hardwood floors, and jump up on the couch next to me. And I'd sit there, beer in one hand as the other scratched her head and stroked her ears, getting a calming and necessary dose of our canine home remedy. Sometimes, she even let me rub the magic lamp of her belly.

The most healing aspect of dogs, I've found, is the simple gift of their presence. They like to be near. They know how to be present.

And as I studied our family's small living, breathing miracle, I realized that it's not necessarily our thoughts and emotions that make us feel more human, but our dogs.

Bijou de Minuit,

CANINE ZEN MASTER, SAYS:

A good dog is as comforting as an old country song backed with a shot of whiskey.

Yes, Your Quirkiness

Given a choice, most dogs would spend their days eating, sleeping, eating, basking in the sun, and eating, with the occasional walk or romp thrown in. Did I mention eating? This preferred canine lifestyle makes the art of dog biography a bit tricky.

Sure, there are all the resonant tales of family legend. But for the angst and drama of every Dead Bird Incident, there are the months and months and *months* of downtime. The narrative thread of Bijou's life spends a lot of time spooled up on her dog bed.

Luckily (for me), Bijou is a prickly bundle of quirks, kinks, and fetishes whose behavior would kindle the eyes of any doggie shrink. She doesn't like being picked up, doesn't like a good brushing, and doesn't like getting dressed up—no pink poodle frocks for her. *And if you think for one minute that you can touch my tail, buster, we're gonna rumble.*

And that's just the beginning. So, here's a look at some of Bijou's most endearing (and not so endearing) quirks.

Lend Me Your Ears (And Toes, While You're at It)

The way our favorite dogs say hello varies from dog to dog. There are the groin greeters (you quickly learn to interpret and intercept that large, happy snout), the dance partners (some big dogs like to place their forepaws on your shoulders and give you a shaggy hug), and the face-washers (hmmm, looks like you missed a spot on your cheek, let me get it for you with my soft, wet salami tongue).

My in-laws' Cavalier King Charles spaniel of blessed memory, K.C., would flip onto his back the moment he saw me, fix me with his huge Marty Feldman eyes, and beg for a belly scratch. And Fern, the apricot cockapoo up the street, either gives me the hard lean against my ankles or plants her petite butt on my foot.

Bijou is an ear-sniffer. When you walk into our house she wants nothing more than to plunge her cold wet nose into your ear, take a big sniff, then perform a fake sneeze. If you'll humor her, she prefers to snuff-sniff both ears.

Offering you the gift of her nose is how Bijou accepts you into her metaphorical wolf pack—and if she's able to prise free a bit of ear funk, that's just a bonus. Bijou's big wet sniff is also a reminder that all of us crave genuine greeting. But to be received in love and kindness, we also need to arrive in love and kindness.

I'm sure that no one wants me to sniff their ears or lick their cheeks—well, *almost* no one—but a real smile and a kind word let people know that we're glad to see them, that we're wagging our spiritual tails.

So, yes, Bijou is a real ear dog. But if she really, really likes you, she also wants to lick your feet.

I know, I know. Some of you are going, "Ewwww, gross," while the foot fetishists among you are going, "Groovy, man." Me? I just find it sweet and primal to be my dog's human salt lick.

When she notices that I have my shoes and socks off, she ambles over, gives my foot a nudge—"Hey, wake up and enjoy this"—and goes to work.

Her little pink tongue slips between my toes, darting in and out like the needle on a sewing machine. She moves methodically down the line, toe to toe, right foot to left foot, absorbed in the task.

It never fails to make me smile, and it does tickle. I'm also moved by the primal animal sweetness of it. Her care of my feet reminds me of how some mother cats will lick their own paws and then groom their kittens.

When Bijou finishes, she gives each foot a loud sniff, making sure she didn't miss any particularly ripe spots, then wanders off.

A couple minutes later, I'll hear her in the kitchen, drinking from her water bowl.

Sleeping Dogs and All That

"Let sleeping dogs lie."

It's one of those warnings we first hear in childhood, but we really don't hear it. We know what it means in a broader sense: "Leave well enough alone," or "Don't stick your nose where it doesn't belong"—are you listening, Bijou?

But you don't understand those words in a profound way until you actually live with a dog. And in Bijou's case, it's a matter of "Let sleeping dogs lie, and her aura, too."

It's uncanny. When Bijou's asleep, if you lower your hand toward her, at the roughly six-inch mark her somnambulant growl, set on simmer, starts. If you pull your hand away, it stops.

If you were actually to touch her as she slept, I suspect, you'd run the risk of going through life known as Three-Finger Jones.

I'm Only Peeing on Your Foot Because I Love You

Maybe it's because her mother didn't teach her any better, or maybe she's just a natural-born snob, but Bijou prefers people to dogs, especially girls and women.

When there's a friendly cluster-sniff in the park, a pack of wagging dogs nose-to-tail-to-nose-to-tail as their leashes tangle in a wicked knot, Bijou is the dog stalking off in the opposite direction:

"Me? In there? Oh, darling, you must have me confused with some member of the pooch peasantry."

Or, "If you don't get your cold, unwelcome snout out of my butt right now you'll spend the rest of your life sniffing with your ears."

With most of the neighborhood dogs, Bijou will deign to offer a cursory "air sniff"—dogs' version of our air kiss—possibly even brushing noses. But within seconds she's doing an end run around Rooney or Charlie, going for the human being who's holding the leash.

Nothing makes her happier than to see our neighbors Harold, Suzanne, and Lacey without their miniature poodle, Charlie. It takes years off her age. She trots up to them, whining in joy, licking cheeks, and sniffing ears. She gets a nice doggie whiff of Charlie, but without the unpalatable fact of his presence. And that means all is perfect in Bijou's world.

It's not so much that she dislikes other dogs, it's that human beings are more up to her keen intellectual standards—well, some of them anyway. She's a Proustian bitch in an Alpo world. And while she isn't averse to pondering the more subtle points of possum dissection, a little Rousseau with that belly-rub will suit her just fine.

As with many small dogs, Bijou's love does sometimes come with a price—another valuable lesson that we human beings have to learn over and over and over.

As any number of women and girls have learned, Bijou will jitterbug for you when you arrive at our house—"I love you! I love you! I love you!"—and lather you with kisses—"I really do! I really do! I really do!"—and then will get so excited, so frenzied, that she will let go and pee on your foot.

"*Biiiiiiii-jouuuuuu!!*"

"But I'm peeing on your foot because I love you."

Doing the Dog

Bijou loves to do the dog.

That's when she spontaneously rolls onto her back and writhes and squirms and scratches her back, groaning in pleasure, her paws scrabbling at the air.

"Do the dog, Biji! Do the dog!"

The broad front hall rug is her preferred spot for this doggie exorcism, as she skritches herself from one end to the other. It does look satisfying, scratching your back on that rug and, I have to admit, there is a part of me that's tempted.

"Do the dog, Dad! Do the dog!"

But I have a feeling that my wife wouldn't approve, and neither would Bijou. That rug is *her* rug, after all.

If there's no rug available, Bijou is happy to do the dog on the lawn, to scratch herself by walking under low, coarse shrubs, and to do the bear by rubbing up against any tree, or leg, that's handy.

I swear that Bijou's eyes light up when she sees me sitting in the den, feet propped up on the ottoman. She passes back and forth beneath my legs, her back purposely scuffing my calves—two times, four times, six times—then she collapses in a heap of sighs and falls asleep.

Yes, this world is made for rubbing.

The Intense Dog Stare

Bijou is the master of the intense dog stare.

Now, this isn't mere, run-of-the-mill begging. This is more canine performance art, tragic doggishness worthy, perhaps, of the Shakespearean stage, or maybe even an Oscar in a lean season.

It's a silent art. She widens her eyes a bit and fixes them on the object of her furry desire, my breakfast bagel, say, or a bowl of Apple Cinnamon Cheerios. But that's just the start.

She lowers her head and flattens her ears so that they are even with her back, and her tail hangs down. And she stares as fiercely as she can. The overall effect is more serpentine than canine, and I, for one, can't help but put words into her mute and firmly shut mouth:

"If we were in the wild, my friend, I'd snap off your hand at the wrist, eat that sandwich, and save your hand for later."

Or, "Fork over those Cheerios, pal, and no one needs to know that this ever happened."

Or, "We're not so different, you and I, we both prefer our roast beef rare."

Or, "You love me, right? Well, show me how much you love me. Prove your love right now, dammit!"

And even though she's putting the touch on us, she doesn't want to be touched. If I try to pet her she shrinks away: "How dare you try to handle me when I'm *emoting*?"

The intense dog stare does not promote proper digestion.

The Thrill of the Chase—Her Tail

It's a bit mortifying to admit—like confessing that you've voted for Ralph Nader for president (I did . . . twice), or, maybe, that your twenty-year-old son collects My Little Ponies (he doesn't, I swear)—but Bijou chases her tail.

It's a cute little shrub of a tail, reminiscent of a clump of broccoli or a small tumbleweed. When she's happy she doesn't really wag it. It's more that it trembles, that she has it on vibrate.

But poor Bijou suffers from tail dysfunction, and sometimes her utterly innocent tail utterly ticks her off.

She'll notice it out of the corner of her eye, like a spy sniffing out shuffles in the shadows, and start in with a steady, low-level growl. If her tail behaves itself, that's it. Bijou throttles down and goes back to sleep.

But if that tail twitches the wrong way or sasses her, she's off: barking and yapping, snarling and yipping—all in pursuit of her tail.

She becomes our momentarily insane whirling poodle dervish, tornadoing around the living room (but somehow never knocking into any furniture), turning and twisting till she squalls herself out and slumps to the floor, heaving and panting.

Sometimes, we'll even find a couple of small scraps of her tail fur on the floor.

Bijou de Minuit,

CANINE ZEN MASTER, SAYS:

Ecclesiastes was right: It's much better to be a living dog than a dead lion—much, much better.

The Obligatory Cat Chapter
Or, a Nod to the Cat Lobby

This is primarily a dog book—with the occasional lizard scurrying through it—but, as we all know, the cat lobby is very powerful. So, with that in mind, this chapter is dedicated to the crazy cats of my childhood—and to all of you cat fanciers out there who are humoring me by nibbling on a dog book.

When and where I grew up, rural New Hampshire in the 1960s, no one went out of the way to get a cat. They just kind of showed up, unbidden, like first frost, the leaves turning, and my great-uncle Allen at suppertime. If you fed it, the cat stayed. If you didn't, it traveled on—just like Uncle Allen.

Blackie, who used to lay out dead mice on our back step as if they were strips of crispy bacon, arrived crying from the tippy-top of a tall pine tree. Rusty, opting for the drowned-rat gambit, showed up at our back door during a thundershower.

My great-grandfather Ora Porter George was a dirt farmer who kept a posse of barn cats to discourage the local rodent riffraff. Those wormy gray-and-white cats were straight out of Central Casting. They were vile and stringy beasts who could've played alley cats—Dead End Cats—in any gangster movie. Being wise and wary children who preferred not to succumb to cat-scratch fever, my sister, Sissy, and I always kept our distance.

Even so, those cats were nowhere near as scary as Grandpa Ora's chickens. Those ornery birds were the yellow-white of an old smoker's fingers, and weren't averse to drawing blood on young and wayward bare legs. They'd peck at the ground, paw at the dirt like feathered bulls, and give you the evil chicken-eye. Brrr.

Sometimes I wondered whether Grandpa Ora's cats and chickens ever racketed and rumbled way after midnight when we were all fast asleep.

As if those cats and chickens weren't bad enough—at least they were *supposed* to be semi-domesticated—there were the yellow-black spiders as big as hubcaps that lurked in the barns and sheds, wrist-thick snakes rustling and slinking through the puckabrush, and rats, raccoons, and skunks that square-danced in the outhouse, making every call of nature an adventure.

Grandpa Ora wasn't the only one in my family who kept cantankerous critters. I grew up in an old-fashioned country town where folks prided themselves on owning dogs that would just as soon shred your throat as look at you, or cats that could perform an emergency appendectomy. It was as if those people somehow transfused the bitterness of their gray and grim lives into their pets.

My great-aunts kept sullen James Dean housecats that had names like Snooky, Tuffy, and Bootsy who popped their claws like switchblades whenever they saw me and Sissy. We preferred the herd of needy kittens over at Grammy Jennings's place, except for her screeching at us: "Don't you handle that cat so much, you'll give it worms." (As far as I can remember, it was only her youngest son, Uncle Junior, who ever got worms.)

Grammy Britton, a gristly vulture named Lilla, always packed a hair-trigger German shepherd, or, in her words, a "police dog." She constantly scolded us kids: "Don't you go teasing that dog now." Grammy Britton, who was my mother's mother, never seemed to notice that her meek little Cerberus always used to slaver at me and Sissy as if we were jumbo pork chops. And Great-Uncle Billy kept a barbaric mutt named Butch whose primary hobby was baring his drooly fangs and tugging his chain taut whenever anyone made the mistake of walking into Uncle Billy's yard. (One subzero night, though, Uncle Billy passed out in a drunken coma before he brought his dog into the house, and the poor pooch froze to death.)

All of those vicious beasts that my relations owned make me wonder how any of us managed to get out of childhood whole. I had a full and active hick boyhood, one that raged with scabs and scrapes, mashed and bloody knees, bumps and lumps, gashes and slashes, jagged glass, ragged steel, knots, knobs, and shiners and, yes, cats' claws and dogs' teeth.

The alpha cat of my youth was Spitz: a consummate mouser, champion swimmer and stealth hitchhiker, who survived car bumpers and getting gut-shot by a .22-caliber rifle before finally using up her nine lives.

Spitz's arrival in our household is the stuff of family legend, is, in fact, downright biblical in the telling.

Dad was out bass fishing one dusk on Long Pond when he saw something swimming furiously toward his canoe. He paddled toward it and, when he got close enough, saw that it was a black kitten that somebody had thrown into the lake to drown, just like baby Moses. He scooped the waterlogged kit up with his bass net just as the shadow of a snapping turtle passed beneath the canoe.

The swimmer Mark Spitz had recently won a clutch of gold medals at the Summer Olympics, so Dad named our new cat Spitz.

Ol' Spitz was an adventurer, kind of the Marco Polo of cats—and she knew how to hitchhike, after a fashion.

Our car at the time was some ancient Detroit glutton—a Buick or an Oldsmobile, I can't quite recall—a gas-guzzling chunk of clunker steel that was as roomy underneath as it was inside.

In the deep heat of summer, Spitz liked to nap under that

car, sometimes even finding nooks in its undercarriage where she'd curl up and go to sleep. Dad knew this, and whenever he drove the car he'd give Spitz time to scoot out and away.

So, one day all six of us piled into the car to go grocery shopping at Custeau's Supermarket, which sat about three miles west of my hometown in Hampstead. A couple of hours after we got home, we realized that we hadn't seen Spitz for a while.

Dad got a funny look on his face and said, "Come with me."

As we rumbled through the twists and turns, hills and gullies of the old Danville Road, Dad said, "I bet that god-damned cat took a ride with us to Custeau's."

Sure enough, we got to the store and found her huddled behind the trash bins, crouched and crying and giving us a what-took-you-guys-so-long look.

We let her ride in the backseat on the way home.

Being an outdoors cat, Spitz rambled freely around the fields and woods of West Kingston, sticking her little black nose where it didn't belong, as cats are wont to do. She eventually fell in with the wrong feline element, probably smoking and gambling and certainly having unprotected premarital sex.

When Spitz had her first, and last, babies—we got her spayed—she once again showed off her knack for finding dark yet comfy hidey-holes. The cloth lining under our musty old overstuffed couch had ripped, creating the perfect entrance to a spot to take a quiet nap or to drop a litter of kittens.

Spitz clandestinely gave birth overnight. When we got up the next morning we could hear her new flock's small yowls, but it took us a while before we peeked under the couch.

I was generally the first one up that summer, rising at five for work. And as I sat at the kitchen table eating my bowl of Frosted Flakes, those kittens would bobble and wobble out from under the couch, crying for breakfast. But Spitz, hiding somewhere, wasn't ready to nurse them yet.

So the kittens—constantly squowling—would nuzzle and gnaw at my ankles, with the more brazen ones climbing up my dungarees with their tiny needle claws.

Miraculously, after they were weaned, we managed to give all the kittens away except for one, Purrcy. Giving away kittens in the country is like trying to give away Canadian pennies—nobody wants them, and you can only do it by sleight of hand.

It's not that kittens aren't cute and that cats aren't decent company. It's the loyalty issue. Let's say you robbed a bank. There's no question that the cat, that fluffy double agent that you clasp to your breast, will turn you in for the reward. Cats only look out for Number One.

But a dog? A dog will happily take the fall with you—and give a lick on the cheek to boot.

Bijou de Minuit,

CANINE ZEN MASTER, SAYS:

Avoid the attic and the cellar—too many stairs are bad for the joints.

The Puppy of Summer

When Owen was seven, he knew he wanted a dog.

He would leave drawings of dogs on our bedroom floor that said, "I want a dog." And he could turn any conversation toward a canine slant.

"How was school today, O-boy?"

"You know my friend Aly Eber?"

"Uh-huh."

"She has three dogs."

Or, "What would you like for breakfast, Owen?"

He'd grin—"I really want a dog."

It was as if Owen understood that his boyhood wouldn't be complete unless he had a dog of his very own.

Meanwhile, as Owen lobbied for a dog, we had all those guinea pigs squealing and multiplying, crafty lizards plotting jailbreaks, and those aristocratic Russian dwarf hamsters pretending that we didn't even exist. But in Owen's mind, all those pets combined didn't come close to equaling one dog.

Well, a boy needs a dog, right? So Deb and I agreed that Owen would get his mutt.

Knowing that there were so many abandoned dogs and cats in this world, as a family we decided to get our dog from a beagle rescue program. We wanted to do the right thing.

Emma—I wanted to call her Faulkner, but got overruled *and* jeered—was a small, sweet beagle, and Owen fell in love with her right away. He wanted nothing more than to have a dog to walk, a dog who'd sleep on his bed.

Within two weeks, he wasn't allowed to touch her.

Emma was scratching herself so much that she started bleeding. We took her to the vet, who took one quick look at her and said, "This is a *sick* dog."

We brought Emma back home, burdened with lotions and antibiotics and the knowledge that none of us was allowed to touch her. She had a skin disease that might be contagious to humans.

Owen was inconsolable. He had his dog, but he couldn't pet her, romp with her, or let her sleep on his bed. Emma would moan and groan and scratch and scratch and *scratch*.

After a couple months of mounting vet bills and owning a quarantined beagle, we all decided that enough was enough. We were tired of being the supporting cast in the sad soap opera "Snoopy Gets Smallpox."

Where the four of us had gone together to pick out Emma, I returned her by myself on a morning ripe with guilt and tears.

She really was a sweet girl.

As Bijou sniffs and snuffs the world this summer as I write, I can't help but wonder whether it's her last.

Where once she was as quick and rambunctious as any dog, she now shuffles and snuffles along, stopping and starting, stopping and starting, as if she's conserving energy. And the steps have become an obstacle to overcome each time she goes out.

But even in slow motion, Bijou relishes her trips outdoors.

"Hey, girl, want to go out?"

She groans to her feet, offers up a couple shakes of her tail, and creaks to the back door. No matter how comfortable you are in the house, dozing on your doggie bed is never better than a sortie outdoors.

Maybe because she arrived in our family in June, I always think of Bijou as a puppy of summer, a furious bunny-lunger always curious to find out whether her practice with dirty socks would work on a skittish rabbit.

She was born on May 5, like my sister-in-law Janet and my niece Amber. I'm not sure it means anything at all, but it's one of those coincidences that makes our family giggle.

There was no particular magic the day we got Bijou.

After our aborted adoption attempt with Emma, we wanted our own puppy. Instead of inheriting somebody else's pet problems, we figured we'd create our own. Deb decided that we'd get a miniature poodle because they're smart—a little *too* smart, if you ask me—don't shed, and she'd had a toy poodle named Monty when she was a kid. Deb is a French teacher, so she also decided that we would name our new dog Bijou de Minuit: Jewel of Midnight.

So the four of us journeyed north of Plattsburgh, New York—Drew was eleven, Owen eight—and fetched our poodle puppy.

All the puppies were impossibly cute—as puppies tend to be—and we picked Bijou because we wanted a female and she seemed a bit more energetic than the other dogs.

"Oh, you'll want to keep an eye on that one," the breeder said to us, almost smirking. "She's the leader of the pack."

Deb and I looked at each other and rolled our eyes. All we saw was a little black fuzz ball nibbling on our sons' fingers.

We soon found out what the breeder had meant. It didn't take Bijou long to try to work and worm her way up in the family hierarchy. Given free rein, Bijou would probably be writing a book about me, instead of me writing a book about her.

Bijou went after Owen first, more specifically his legs. We all know that male dogs like to muckle ahold of a nice stout tibia and, uh, say hello. We weren't quite prepared for a female poodle puppy who also dabbled in that hobby. And Drew and Owen's bust-a-gut laughter didn't help matters any, either.

We finally broke Bijou of lusting after legs, but she still ended up making Owen her boy. It was Owen who started feeding her from the table, starting Bijou down the long road of begging and thieving.

She still begs, but these days Bijou gives the bunnies a half-hearted lurch, just enough to make them hop off, their white tails flashing in disdain. Satisfied that the rabbits still understand the prey-predator relationship, she dodders on.

Each season serves up its own peculiar delight to catch a dog's fancy: Fireflies in summer and snowflakes in winter, brittle leaves come fall, and convocations of robins in spring. All those things are meant to be snapped at, barked at, and, perhaps, tasted.

But it's Bijou's nose that knows summer best.

She keeps it flush to the sidewalk—sniff, sniff, sniff—searching for the remains of Popsicles and ice-cream cones, thrusts it into shrubs for signs of her neighborhood buddies, or periscopes it into the air, wet nostrils flaring, trying to determine what mysteries of aroma are wafting through our block, wafting through her life.

Bijou de Minuit,

CANINE ZEN MASTER, SAYS:

Possession—especially anything gripped in your mouth—really *is* nine-tenths of the law.

"You Take the Dog Out, I Have Cancer"

Funny stuff happens when you have cancer. Seriously.

The classic family one-liner that stems from me having cancer is this: "You take the dog out. I have cancer." That soon morphed into infinite variations, along the lines of: "Can I sit in that chair? I have cancer," or "Do you mind switching from HGTV to the Patriots game? I have cancer."

So, please, read this book and buy two or three more for family and friends. I had cancer.

Yeah, "You take the dog out, I have cancer." It is one of those wonderful and mundane things. Even if you or someone in your family has cancer or some other serious illness, the dog still has to go out. But rather than being a burden, it's a gesture toward the possibility that life can once again be normal.

Other funny stuff happens, too, and not necessarily of the canine slant.

Take the winter when I was in the middle of hormone

therapy and radiation for my cancer. One of my relatives came by the house and said: "You know, if you need any weed to get you through this, I know where to get it. And my friends only smoke really, really good dope."

After politely declining—I was truly and deeply touched—I just cracked up. The laughter and the tears made me feel better than any amount of marijuana would have. All I could imagine was this relative getting busted and then pleading, "But, officer, I'm copping this for a guy who has cancer."

As I recovered from cancer surgery, treatment, and its aftermath, it was important to me to try to see the absurd plaid lining in a difficult situation. Just because the stakes with cancer are dark and mortal that doesn't mean there aren't moments of high hilarity. You have to laugh when you have cancer, or you'll end up being devoured.

Being able to laugh (and walk the dog) in the face of cancer lets you continue to own yourself, as hard as that might be, rather than ceding ownership to the disease. A good laugh and a good dog remind you that you are not your cancer.

After surgery, I was urinating blood, my testicles swelled to the size of shot-puts, I had drains hanging from my body that the nurses called "grenades" (because of their shape), and it hurt to laugh.

But I laughed, anyway, because there was a certain earthy humor to all these bodily insults. And in telling these stories to my friends with a grin after the fact, I could let the listener know that I'd journeyed to a narrow place of darkness, but had come back.

There's a part of me that would like nothing better than to do cancer stand-up comedy—please cue up a neurotic, put-upon Rodney Dangerfield voice:

"So, there I am, half-naked in a dimly lit room, my feet are bound, and cool female hands are manipulating my body. Yeah, it was great. I was getting prepped for the radiation machine."

Or: "You know, a funny thing happened on the way to the cancer institute this morning. Just a quarter-mile from the institute, my wife and I got stuck in traffic behind a truck . . . a casket truck: 'Batesville Casket Company: A Hillenbrand industry, helping families honor the lives of those they love.' At least it wasn't following me . . . with vultures on top."

I know that sometimes laughter seems impossible. After my cancer diagnosis I plunged into a bleak funk. And then there was the struggle with a post-treatment depression that left my days swaddled in wearying grays.

But no matter how remorseless the gloom, we humans tend to have our antennae for humor out. We *are* the animal that wants to laugh—and dogs are among the animals that help us laugh—wants to unlock itself through a chuckle and a chortle. And laughter lets us cope, even in awkward moments.

There was the time when a colleague gave me the get-well gift of a book. Being a wiseguy (maybe I should blame it on the hormone therapy), I cracked, "Oh, great, it's probably '1,000 Places to See Before You Die.'"

My colleague gasped, then blushed as she handed me a copy of "1,000 Recordings to Hear Before You Die." We both laughed (and I apologized for wising off). But she only laughed after I laughed first.

In my laughter, I've been able to nudge my family and friends into laughing, into letting them thaw their tight and frozen faces. And that's important, too, because when you're seriously ill, you're not the only one who needs to heal.

Oh, and as long as you're still here, could you please take the dog out?

Bijou de Minuit,

CANINE ZEN MASTER, SAYS:

Never pass up the chance to

pounce on a sock.

Loki, International Cat of Mystery

In her latter-day creakiness, Bijou likes nothing better than to settle into a sunny patch of grass to doze and graze as Deb gardens.

And, it seems to us, that once Bijou groans, sighs, and squirms herself into contentment, that's the cue for Loki, the slinky black cat of our neighbors the Gills, to stroll into our backyard and stretch out about, oh, three feet from Bijou and stare.

Loki, named for the Norse god of mischief (who was also the wicked archenemy of the Mighty Thor in the Marvel comic book), is our neighborhood's international cat of mystery. He's a classic Halloween of a black cat, and would make a fine hood ornament on the broomstick of any moon-bound witch.

I rarely see Loki run. He's the master of the feline sashay, the quick brush of your legs, and a thousand-yard stare that percolates up from the depths of his yellow-green eyes.

We never quite know where Loki's going to show up. When he's not taunting the dogs next door—Annie and Rooney—you can find him flush to a curb (daring any vehicle to park) or lurking under a shrub, practicing his inscrutable cat glance. Sometimes he uses our stoop as his own personal hoodlum street corner, smoking Lucky Strikes, whistling at the girl cats as they wriggle past, and sometimes trying to zip into our house. Our neighborhood is Loki's oyster.

Most often, I'll see him in the morning, sauntering around the corner of our garage with the air of a sharp-clawed mammal that's just committed some act of mayhem.

Lord Loki looks up: "Oh . . . hello, Dana."

"Hello, Loki."

Then Loki skulks past in the attitude of "Ask me no questions, and I'll tell you no lies."

Despite his metaphorical switchblade and leather jacket, Loki does sometimes lose his cool. As I walked into our backyard one afternoon, at least twenty birds were roosting in the trees and throwing a fit. The crows were cawing, the blue jays were jawing, and the sparrows were sparring. We had all caught Loki red-pawed . . . and red-mouthed.

He was hunched over a dead baby rabbit and did not look happy to see me. He grabbed the rabbit by the neck, slipped out of the yard, across the street, and into the privacy of his own bushes—all cat, all predator, and totally ruffled.

But not all prey is quite so passive. As I looked out of my

study window one fall morning, I saw Loki sprinting across the street—and he never runs, unless he has to—with a bull raccoon built like a South African rugby player right on his tail, literally. (Maybe that raccoon's name was Thor.) Loki, apparently, had ignored Bijou's dictum about never ticking off any animal that outweighs you by more than two-to-one.

When it comes to Bijou, Loki stares long enough and hard enough for her to wake up. And once he has elicited the mandatory bark, growl, or leash-jerk, Loki gathers himself and wanders off, tail switching and twitching as it waves goodbye.

Bijou de Minuit,

CANINE ZEN MASTER, SAYS:

Human beings say, "Follow the money."

But dogs know that it's much smarter

to "follow the food."

One Name Is Never Enough: The Nicknames

There's just something about our mercurial pooches that invites additional names, ones that capture them in their different attitudes. From minute to minute, dogs are as changeable as the weather atop Mount Everest and their arsenal of names needs to reflect that.

Monet had his haystacks that he painted over and over, and I have a dog that I name over and over. Here are a few of my favorites for Bijou.

Peaches She's Peaches at her most vibrant, when she dances on her hind legs or skitters after a ball on the kitchen linoleum. It's best said in an exuberant, high-pitched voice: "*Peeea-ches!*"

Dogzilla This is the dog who growls in her sleep as your hand nears her head, who gives you the "if-we-were-in-the-wild-I-could-rip-out-your-throat-and-devour-you" look, who found one loose corner, then tore up a patch of the kitchen linoleum. And, yes, given a chance, she could probably destroy an accurate scale model of Tokyo. *Variation:* Twenty-three Pounds of Fury—that's the dog dressed in a black duster, sporting mirror-shade goggles, and riding sidecar to a Harley.

Muffin or **Muffy** Screeched in the same attitude as "*Peeea-ches!*"

Weasel Weasel is the dog who stalks bunnies and squirrels, who slinks through the rain, who slips socks and underwear out of the laundry basket, who sits patiently in the kitchen when Deb is baking, waiting for the stray Nestle's butterscotch morsel that might bounce her way. *Also:* Weezy and Weezer.

Poodle-Puss It just sounds funny, like platypus: "Come here, Poodle-Puss," or "Want a treat, Poodle-Puss?" A variation on the old cartoon character—"Exit, stage left"—Snagglepuss.

Wolfie Girl Inspired by the Beach Boys' song "Surfer Girl." "Wolfie girl, ooooo, you're my little Wolfie girl." It's also a reminder, as improbable as it may seem, that my neurotic miniature poodle is a cousin to wolves.

Her Grumpiness Some days Bijou is simply regal, beautiful, and . . . grumpy, having gotten up on the wrong side of the dog bed. I suspect that the British royals have the same problem with Queen Elizabeth. *Variation:* Her Creakiness.

Snurly Gurly This is our dog who is always curly, and sometimes snarly. *Also:* Your Snurliness, sometimes, inexplicably, evolving into Snively or Slimely or Stoatly.

Biji Shakespeare had his "Dark Lady," and I have my dark-haired Biji, almost rhymes with Fiji. Sometimes I believe that one of the things that makes us human is the ability to take any name and make a diminutive of it. I would bet any number of dog biscuits that King Nebuchadnezzar's mother called him "Nebby."

Curly-Haired Bitch My wife, Deb, has dark curly hair—perhaps explaining her affinity for poodles. So when Bijou is barking nonstop at the upstairs window at trespassers both real and imagined (and if I feel like baiting the neighbors), I'll bellow: "Shut up, you curly-haired bitch!" Bijou doesn't stop barking, but it sure makes the humans in the house laugh.

Wonder Wart-Dog As Bijou aged, she started growing bright red warts on her delicate body. The warts were harmless enough but generally elicited big, long "*ewwwws*" from Deb and the boys. They reminded me, though, of a long-forgotten comic book character from my errant childhood, Wonder Wart-Hog (the Hog of Steel). Thus the nickname Wonder Wart-Dog was born.

Doogie Bowser, M.D. (Medical Dog) Dr. Bowser is the dog who dutifully made house calls each morning when Owen and I were sick: Cold nose poked in the ear, temperature looks good. Silky ear pressed to the chest, heart and lungs are working. Plaintive paw resting on the wrist, pulse is strong. And if you stuck out your tongue, Dr. Bowser would lunge for it with her own—our dog, the happy tongue depressor.

Little Whiskers McGee She's Little Whiskers McGee when she's scruffy and scrappy—a Little Rascals sort of mutt—as she stalks socks and bunnies and jumble cookies.

Little Miss Mojo She's Little Miss Mojo at her most mysterious. When she stares into space or speaks in tongues in her sleep or when her groans sound as deep as the moan of a ramshackle pier in an ocean storm. And she's Little Miss Mojo when she snugs next to me as I listen to the primal blues and plaints of Muddy Waters, Little Walter, and Howlin' Wolf.

Optional Prefix Most any nickname can be intensified by adding the prefix "Daddy's little": "Ohhh, Daddy's little Dogzilla," or "Aww, look at Daddy's little Weasel." The more you sound like the village idiot discussing Socrates or Nietzsche with a chipmunk, the more effective the prefix.

Bijou de Minuit,

CANINE ZEN MASTER, SAYS:

Most any bed is just the

right size for two adults

and a pooch.

There's No Time but the Present: Finding My Inner Dog

Dogs live in the eternal present. To Bijou, it's always *now*. Feed me *now*. Take me out now. Scratch my head *now*. Let me catch that bunny *now*.

She doesn't think about that other family that almost took her home in 1997. She doesn't wonder whether her mother loved her enough. She doesn't worry about her retirement doghouse.

She simply *is*. She instinctively knows that this world is for licking and looking, for snuffling and pawing and listening. She knows that this world is right *now*, this very fleeting moment.

And that was a strong lesson for me as I recovered from prostate cancer.

As I lay on my post-op sickbed, Bijou taught me that the one best moment is the one we occupy right now . . . and now . . . and *now*—and while we're here, could you scratch my ears just a bit down and to the right? Thanks.

It doesn't pay to obsess over the past the way Bijou sometimes worries her paws wet. And if you fret too much over the future, you fritter away the present.

Simply put, Bijou has helped me find my inner dog.

We are both resolute believers in the restorative powers of naps, walks, and nesting in the den. And while I don't like having my ears scratched, as she does, it does feel good when someone rubs my buzz cut—I get the "three-zero" blade these days, complete with a hot-lather shave, at Balonze Barber Shop.

Bijou especially guided me toward understanding my doggie self after I had cancer surgery, followed by radiation and hormone therapy.

After surgery, I was reduced to a helpless animal state. I needed to be fed and watered. And, when you're walking the hospital halls, your IV pole is effectively a leash. Bijou and I have both wrestled with issues of incontinence—though I swear that I never peed on anyone's foot.

When I got home from the hospital, Deb, Drew, and Owen took me for walks, just as they did Bijou. I managed, however, not to bark and growl at the other dogs in the neighborhood or scarf up desiccated worms off the sidewalk.

During hormone therapy I literally was as hungry as a dog—no offense meant to any of you canine readers out there—which gave the two of us plenty of culinary common ground. We both shared an unhealthy affection for Cool

Ranch Doritos, and Bijou taught me that if someone is eating something you like—an Italian sub, say—it never hurts to ask: "Are you going to finish that?"

I also learned that cancer time and dog time aren't so different. We know that our dogs' lives are compressed into ten to fifteen years, that their brilliant flames burn even more quickly than our own. Time is compressed, too, when you have cancer, and after. Once you've been seriously ill, you can't take ten years from now for granted, or next year for that matter.

Each morning these days, Bijou and I ease outside and troll the sidewalk. She likes to poke along because there are trees and bushes to sniff for new messages, acorns and bird berries to taste, dew to lick off the grass, and His Feline Arrogance, Lord Loki, with whom to share inscrutable stares.

As Bijou does her business, I sniff the air and ponder the weather, fetch my neighbor's newspaper and toss it onto her porch, and also share inscrutable stares with Loki, sometimes complemented by a quick belly-scratch that Loki assumes is his lordly due as the block's feline tollbooth. Afterward, Bijou takes her pills (hidden in mini-pepperoni), and I take my pills (gulped with orange juice).

There's no question that these days I possess—or, perhaps, am possessed by—an inner dog.

I still grunt, yowl, and tussle with my sons. This isn't as mean as it sounds, given that they're both in their twenties, well over six feet tall, and that Drew is a former captain of Dartmouth College's championship rugby team.

I sheepishly admit that I still sniff the occasional dirty sock—it still fascinates me how funky socks reek like old corn chips—but, unlike Bijou, I don't try to break the sock's imaginary neck.

Like Bijou, I growl if you try to wake me from a sound sleep. Of course, I don't get the twenty-plus hours a day of snooze time that she requires, not that I'm against that idea.

Sleep, in fact, is our great common denominator. We both believe that naps are the absolute core, the source, of a full life. We both have the uncanny ability to nap anywhere, anytime, though only Bijou has the knack to bounce and bound wide awake when she senses the presence of pepperoni pizza.

We both snore like Gemini rockets blasting off. Sometimes, after midnight, when I can't sleep I hear Bijou rumbling in the kitchen—the small canine furnace who warms our lives.

The sun and the wind complete Bijou's trifecta for what's needed to live the ideal life. She spends her days following the sun—from bed to bed, from window to window—in pursuit of the perfect swatch of sun. And when she finds it, she stretches out to her full length, groans and sighs in pleasure, and falls asleep in the blessing of the sunlight.

Who can dispute her?

Then there's the wind. There's nothing like a day that

breaks with the leaves rushing and riffling like a river, when wind-goaded dust devils whirl up and down the street, when wind clouds bruise the sky black-and-blue.

Bijou thrusts her snout into the air, nostrils flaring, tail quaking. It's as if she's parsing the entire world in the windy currents coursing through our neighborhood.

And I totally understand. Windy days make me giddy, harry me back to my childhood, where gusts make the curtains shimmy, where the wind bears the haunting news of the Boston & Maine moaning toward the North Country, where the snow is beaten into whipped-cream snowdrifts, and where the skeletal oaks of autumn rasp and rattle.

Like most dogs, Bijou is all nose. But I am, too. If you can't sniff this world, it's not worth living in. What's better than the damp-cellar musk of a vintage science fiction paperback? Or the hot-rubber reek of a stock car bellowing around a racetrack? Or the earthy funk of your very own rain-soaked mutt?

When we're out and about, Bijou likes people better than other dogs, as I've said, and I like dogs better than other people. And, probably most important, we've come to understand our shadow selves.

Bijou is an old lady as I write. She holds court from her bed, she sighs a lot, she knows pain, her medication has made her gain weight and some of her hair is falling out. (I've experienced all those symptoms, too.)

But despite the aches and pains of old age, Bijou is still game. She still trots after her ball, still hobbles up the steps to bark at the front door when a visitor comes calling, still does the backyard bunny-lunge. And some of that rebellious fur has grown back, darker than the rest, and looks like a map of Africa if you squint. The rambunctious puppy still lives in her doggie heart.

There are times when I've felt puppy-like, too. That first afternoon of my prostate-cancer surgery, as I phased in and out of consciousness, my family hovered around my bed, smiling and encouraging. There was a part of me that felt as if I were a new puppy, being brought home in a box.

And, I have to admit, I had an atavistic impulse to gently lick somebody's hand. Just like a brand-new puppy, it took me a few post-op days to fully find my legs. When you're recovering, all petting and rubbing is acceptable—no belly-rubs, though, when you have had abdominal surgery.

As I said, Bijou and I spend a lot of time in the den. I like it at night, as I'm reading, when she wakes from a nap, stands up, shakes off the sleep, then hobbles over to me. She brushes against me a couple times, as if to make sure that I'm awake, then rests her chin on the cushion of my chair, asking to be scratched on the head.

So often, we—dogs and humans—just need to be near each other. We need the presence of another heartbeat, the inhale and exhale of another soul. Dogs understand the healing power of having your skull kneaded, and constantly raise their heads toward our ready hands.

We humans like it, too. I never say no when Deb or the boys want to rub my fresh buzz cut—good dog that I am.

Bijou de Minuit,

CANINE ZEN MASTER, SAYS:

If a big dog wants to eat your food,

just bow your head, do-si-do around him,

and go and finish off his bowl.

The Ten Dog Commandments

I know, I know, Moses, Mount Sinai, and the stone tablets get all the hype and publicity commandment-wise—and deservedly so, I guess.

But most people don't know about the Ten Dog Commandments. My copy was slipped to me by Vinnie, a pug of the canine variety, from Bayonne, New Jersey. (Vinnie's a "human whisperer.") These commandments weren't carved in stone, but were carefully printed on the brown inside of an old Purina Dog Chow sack. I think it's an authentic document.

The Ten Dog Commandments

1. I am your D_g, who brings you out of the house in the pouring rain and in the freezing cold. You shall have no other dogs before me.

2. You shall not make for yourself room for a cat. For I, your D_g, am a jealous dog. (OK, OK, if you really need a cat, too, let's talk about it. Deal?)
3. You shall not make wrongful use of the name of your D_g. When you find a chunk ripped from a thawing steak or a puddle of urine on the kitchen floor, do not say, "Where's that goddamned Lassie," but say, "I wonder how that happened?" (D_g only knows, right?)
4. Remember, to a dog every day is a Sabbath of rest. So let's keep it holy together.
5. Honor all the dogs in your midst, the mothers and the fathers and the puppies, so that the days of you and your D_g(s) may be long.
6. You shall not murder a dog. (This, of course, goes without saying, but I'm saying it anyway—better safe than sorry. Dog fights aren't so hot, either.)
7. You shall not romp with an alien dog—unless your dog grants you permission.
8. You shall not steal a dog. (But a cat? *No problem*. Cats just *love* to be stolen, the same way they just *live* to climb trees and ford deep rivers.)
9. You shall not bear false witness against your D_g. A dog has never *actually* eaten anybody's homework.
10. You shall not covet your neighbor's dog. (Your neighbor's spouse, OK, but never the dog. That's just plain wrong.)

Bijou de Minuit,

CANINE ZEN MASTER, SAYS:

One dog is good,

two is even better,

and three is heavenly.

Self-Medicating with the Bark Club

Sometimes I think that Bijou's bundle of poodle eccentricities is just her way of self-medicating. The poor little thing is as high-strung and swoony as any Southern belle pining and wasting away in some humid, vine-strangled Gothic mansion.

But Bijou doesn't have recourse to the usual cures: obsessive sex, bourbon and Cokes, morphine, voodoo. So she resorts to tail-chasing, paw-licking, barrage barking, and all the other quirks I've already mentioned.

One of Bijou's most tender quirks is the begging snork. This happens when she gets impatient. If she decides that we're not slipping her that bagel crumb, sliver of roast beef, or Cheez Doodle in a timely manner, she gathers herself and lets loose with a fake sneeze, a loud snork that coats our legs in a fine glaze of poodle nasal mist that's not quite as beguiling as Chanel wafting from an atomizer.

Then there's the barrage barking.

All dogs bark, of course. That's part of the deal. Telling a dog not to bark is like persuading a Republican lawyer not to join a country club—it's just about impossible.

But barrage barking is some kind of canine warfare. It's bombs being dropped from B-52s. It's depth charges plunging into the ocean. It's bazookas homing in on tanks. It's a bark that speaks of fire and intruders, a barking to herald the end of the world.

Or, maybe, it's Phil Spector's Wall of Sound. And on it goes—*bark, bark, bark*—until every room has been blessed with a bark—*bark, bark, bark*—until everyone in the neighborhood indeed knows that Bijou's home—*bark, bark, bark*—until Bijou barks herself out and falls asleep. *Snore, snore, snore* . . .

I bet it feels good to bark like that, though, to let loose with all your strength, to say to the world: "I'm here! I'm here! I'm *goddamn* here!"

Most of the time, Bijou's barking is more normal as she takes part in the neighborhood's canine rituals. It doesn't take much to incite our local bark club: the mail truck lurching and squealing to a halt, a strange pooch strolling by, a baby squalling.

It's often Rooney, a Tibetan terrier, or Annie, a feisty and mouthy schnauzer, who stirs the pot, who lays down the bass line: "Bark, bark, bark. Bark, bark, bark." Then Bijou, who has never been a dog to pass up an opportunity to speak, starts in—"ruff-ruff, ruff-ruff"—the squeak buried in her bark getting higher pitched the longer she goes. Bijou's bark is then seconded by Charlie, the mini-poodle who lives behind us, the two of them reinforcing each other in call-and-response.

Within a minute the whole neighborhood is engulfed in howls, yowls, and growls, in yips and yaps. Riley, a pink-nosed shepherd mix, weighs in with his Barry White–deep "woof . . . woof." Maddy, the resident basset hound and escape artist who's an expert at digging under fences, pitches in with her dolphin-like baying. Lola, a white feather-duster of a mutt, offers up her muted "reep-reep."

And if you tilt your ear just so, you can also hear Pickles, a kung-fu shih tzu who has a ponytail and an attitude—"yap, yap, yap"—and Fern, the sweet apricot cockapoo who leans hard against your leg if she likes you—"yip, yip, yip."

(Fern, by the way, does the best "snake" I've ever seen a dog do. She lies flat, her chin and belly flush to the grass, then hitches herself forward, creeping and slinking, looking for all the world like the rare and treasured apricot cockapoo snake. We dog lovers live for these moments.)

It's as if Frank Zappa were still alive and conducting a makeshift canine chorus, a regular bark-annalia.

Then it's over as fast as it started. There are naps to be resumed, panting tongues to be watered, grass to be nibbled.

The street quiets down . . . and you might hear the Harras triplets, three boys, carousing in their backyard. Oddly enough, the Harrases don't own a dog.

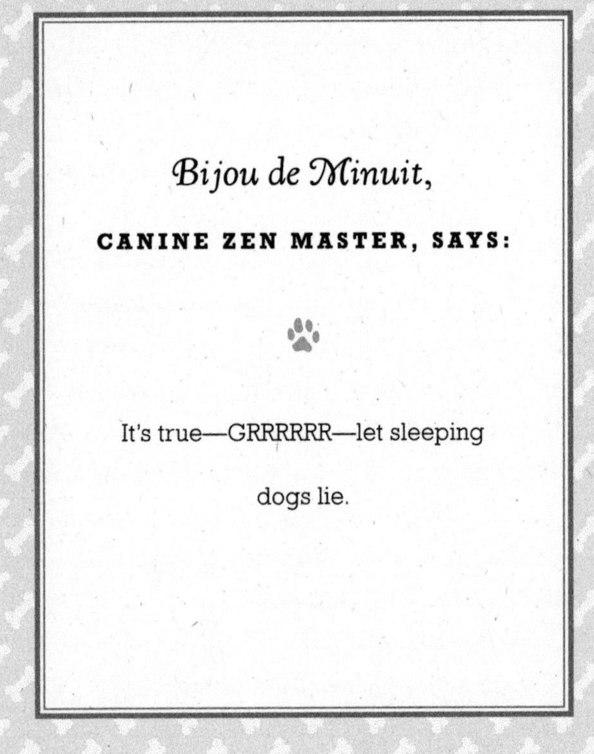

Bijou de Minuit,

CANINE ZEN MASTER, SAYS:

It's true—GRRRRRR—let sleeping dogs lie.

Other Dogs, Other Lives

The memories of former dogs have the power to carry us back to their place and time, no matter how many decades have passed.

When I conjure my first memory—of Midnight licking my face as I stood in my crib—I'm back at our first place, a ramshackle husk of a house that'd once been a small rural shoe factory. A run-down rent house gnawed at by rats and acres and acres of swampy puckabrush, it only had cold running water for plumbing (we had an outhouse for a toilet), no central heat, and the flimsy white curtains that would waltz in the wind. And I can tell you from long experience that a good and loyal dog is a strong gift when you don't have much money.

Our next dog after Midnight, King, was a mutt built like a fullback. He loved my old man and spent his days digging craters in our dooryard, before settling into them to sleep.

When Dad got home from work at the furniture factory,

King would lurch awake and jump on him so hard that sometimes he knocked him down, and Dad was more or less built like King. I swear that I almost remember the old man rocking and bucking on that dog's back as if it were a bronco.

My folks gave King away after deciding that he was too rowdy a dog to have with three small children.

Twinkles is one of the ghosts of my childhood. She was a sleek black bitch with a white starburst on her forehead. One season we had her, the next she was gone. We were going through tough times, and Mom and Dad said we couldn't afford to keep her. They gave her to a family that owned a farm. (There were a lot more farmers way back then.)

By the time of Twinkles and King, we had moved to another house, on New Boston Road. It was a step up from our old place—it actually had a flush toilet instead of an outhouse—but the only running water was still cold and sometimes rusty. It was framed on one side by Route 125, the main road through Kingston, the power-line road on the other, and backed by a stumpy swamp infested with snakes, mosquitoes, and snapping turtles.

When I think about that house nowadays, I hear the squirrels sprinting and hurdling around the attic, smell the swamp funk from down back, see the monarch butterflies swarming the milkweed patch.

That house, with its porch and rickety and feral barn, is the heart of my childhood, where I fell in love with books, wrote my first stories, decided I was going to go to college. And the porch became my studio, where you'd find me writing and drawing and reading as Boston Red Sox baseball games snapped, crackled, and popped from the Sylvania radio that had the broken, upside-down S.

It was also where Tiny would sleep with me on the spare steel cot on summer nights.

Tiny was the dog who finally managed to stick. He didn't get hit by a car, had a sweet face, and didn't eat too much. There were no farms in his future.

Grammy Jennings gave him to us, an ungainly son of her wicked Chihuahua, Nipper (who prided himself on living up to his nasty little name), and a serene terrier mix named Lady. With parents like that, ol' Tiny was one funny-looking mutt: smallish, and all ears and nose. But he was ours. He was mine.

Tiny was an indoors-outdoors dog. (My parents, being no-nonsense country folk, didn't believe in pets who lived exclusively indoors—hell, we had relations who didn't live exclusively indoors.) He spent nights in the house and days outside, hooked up to a healthy length of chain.

Bringing him in at night, though, always felt like an adventure, especially when I was younger. We kept Tiny staked at the far side of the barn, toward the gloomy and forbidding swamp. And one of the unspoken house rules was that the dog didn't get to come in until the very last dot of light had been blotted from the Western sky.

Most folks don't know it nowadays, but it gets really, really dark way out in the boonies. And even if you grow up in the country, you never get quite used to it.

Not surprisingly, I suppose, I suffered from a fevered, hyperactive imagination. Tiny's lair was only maybe twenty yards from the back door, but it lay in deep darkness once the sun went down. You can cue up the eerie theremin music right now, gentlemen.

I'd creep outside, feet crunching on the dirt driveway, the kitchen lights shining feebly through the windows.

"Tiny?"

I'd hear his chain rattle as he shook himself awake. But was it just Tiny out there? That clattering chain sounded like Tiny. But maybe it was an escaped convict from the County Farm in Brentwood, or some marsh ghost, or, heck, even Injun Joe from *Tom Sawyer*. Then there was the possibility of my dog being held captive by skunks or snakes, or fisher cats, or maybe even a stray wolverine.

"Tiny?"

Rattle-rattle.

(Timber rattlers don't sound like steel chain, right?)

My heart ratcheted up and adrenaline appropriately boosted, I'd dash around the corner of the barn, unhook Tiny, and be off to the house before his chain jangled to the ground, the dog at my heels. I'm sure Tiny wondered what all the rush was about, but he never let on.

Sleeping on the porch was the best part of summer. Nothing could beat the sharp night air, the Red Sox of Carl Yastrzemski and Tony Conigliaro sputtering from the radio and Tiny snoring at my feet. By morning, though, he'd always manage to worm his way under the covers.

In winter, there was no pretense. The second floor of our house wasn't heated or insulated. Frost devils capered on the insides of my bedroom windows, and I could see my breath when I woke up in the morning.

Tiny would wriggle under the covers and we'd snuggle against the arctic blast. Before we fell asleep he'd give me a quick lick on the cheek, as if to say: "You keep me warm, and I'll keep you warm, OK?" Such is the basis for basic mammalian trust.

I have to admit, though, as Tiny snored on the pillow next to mine, it was kind of like sleeping with a very funny looking kid brother who had a cold black nose.

Bijou de Minuit,

CANINE ZEN MASTER, SAYS:

Never go around an object that blocks your path. Rub up against it and scratch your back.

The Holiness of Dogs

My friend Anne Laurent, who is studying to be a rabbi, once said to me: "Start with the dog. If you start with the dog, before you know it, you're dealing with the Big Picture."

I agree with her. Strangely enough, if you can manage to make the world small enough—say, the size of a miniature poodle—it becomes the universe.

I think that one of the reasons we're so taken by our dogs is that we intuitively understand that each dog is its own creation story. Dogs don't live the questions, they're our loving answers.

Simply put: Dogs are holy.

Most religious traditions tell us that we should be able to see this holiness in each other, that each one of our faces is, in fact, the face of God. But there are so many complications, right? That guy is too ugly, that one is too smug, and he's a bully. That woman is vain, that one's the size of a sperm whale, and she's a battle-ax.

But, for some reason, when we look at a good dog, all we see is its true and pure self, its holiness.

And that's why I despise the whole dog and master setup.

I know, I know, we can't have our dogs roaring, romping, and rampaging through our homes and neighborhoods. But I bristle at some people's insistence that dogs should be bent to our flawed human wills.

Blind obedience is no virtue in a dog. The stroll from the rarefied airs of a dog show to the dark pits of a dog fight is a short one.

One of the important lessons that our years with Bijou has reinforced is that human beings are not the center of existence. Spend any time among animals—both wild and domestic—and the supreme arrogance of our species becomes intolerable and embarrassing.

In the deepest sense, Bijou is not my dog, is not our dog. She is a fellow creature on this uncertain journey. We invited her into our home and have cared for her, even as she has cared for us in her holiness.

I'm touched by this sense of holiness whenever I see a three-legged dog. I'm always impressed by their pluck. It's as if they don't even know that they only have three legs. They still want to carouse and cavort, get fresh with dogs of the opposite sex, bark, and take a walk. When I see a dog with three legs, part of me smiles in admiration, and part of me wants to cry in joy at its determination.

And it seems to me, by the way, that most every small town in America has a three-legged dog named Lucky.

As I write, it's a humid summer morning, and Bijou is napping on the cool floor in the back hall. Her body rises and falls with the bellows of her lungs as she sleeps, wheezing—like an ancient Ford trying to start up on a cold winter morning.

Every few minutes her back legs jitter, toenails tapping out secret dog code on the floor. Then there's the brief "woof . . . woof," even as she keeps right on snoozing. But she's just a dog, right? Just a dog.

I don't think so.

Here we are, orphans in the vast cosmos as *our* planet dervishes around *our* sun. We skate on the surface of a deep mystery in a constantly expanding universe of black holes and dark matter, of galaxies dying and galaxies being born, of an Unknown that could drive a man mad if he thought about it too much.

And amid all that cosmic strangeness—how unlikely—a dog: a Divine candle with her humid doggie breath.

Bursting with the biological urgency of life, her unlikely light is a hedge against the bleak and blank entropy that we are told will one day be faced by us, the Earth, even the universe.

But Bijou is still asleep, still wheezing. And I am somehow comforted.

Bijou de Minuit,

CANINE ZEN MASTER, SAYS:

Good things come

to she who waits—especially

in the kitchen.

Being There

We never have to worry about dogs being there for us.

It's in their makeup. Dogs want to be there. They are part of the pack, the family. Bijou is no lone poodle. She prefers company, especially that of my wife, especially in the kitchen.

Deb likes to bake, and Bijou likes to pretend to be the baker's helper. She's a poodle who doesn't mind a fine dusting of Gold Medal flour on her fur. Part of this, to be sure, is Bijou's lust for sweet, fat prey. You never know when a smattering of butter will plop to the floor or a clatter of chocolate morsels—*mmmm, semisweet.*

But, more than anything, she wants to be there with Deb as she mixes and kneads, measures sugar and flour, and cracks eggs. Sometimes sitting, sometimes flopped on the floor, sometimes underfoot—"Bijou, are you trying to kill me?"—but *there*, always there.

And when Deb heads upstairs—stairs are a challenge for

Bijou these days—she comes looking for me. She peers around the corner from the kitchen and into the dining room to determine whether I'm hanging out in the den. Then it's *click, click, click* across the hardwood floors to my chair.

I tip her for her presence with some quick head-scritches, then she curls up a couple feet away, satisfied to be there, to be near.

When our house was full, Bijou made her rounds each night, part official greeter, part night watchman, checking in on Drew and Owen as they did their homework, Deb as she prepared for classes the next day, and me as I read or listened to music.

She'd give each one of us a friendly nudge, maybe lie down for a few minutes, then move on—a dog at work because she wanted to be.

And the summer I recovered from cancer surgery, at least a couple times a day she'd leap up onto my sickbed and curl up at my feet. Her presence, her *being there*, was a better tonic for me than any get-well card. And she did the same for Owen as he recovered from his lung operations and liver failure.

Who knew, when we got her back in 1997, what a tender difference Bijou would make in our lives?

Bijou de Minuit,

CANINE ZEN MASTER, SAYS:

Sigh when the spirit moves you.

Sometimes a deep sigh is better

than a prayer.

I, Dog Nurse

Welcome to another taut and thrilling episode of *Bijou's Anatomy.*

Bijou has an impressive medicine chest for a twenty-three-pound miniature poodle. Each day she takes phenobarbital to prevent seizures, Proin for incontinence, a microdose of amoxicillin to prevent her chronic urinary tract infections, and tramadol and prednisone to mute her back pain—all of them wrapped in slices of mini-pepperoni. Then there's the daily prune for regularity, the silver sulfadiazine salve for her warts, not to mention the monthly heartworm pill and the antibiotic wash for her sensitive ears. Bijou tends to attract bacteria the way other dogs attract fleas.

All of this raises an important question: Just how did dogs manage to survive before they domesticated us?

But given that Bijou helped bring me back to health when I was sick, it's only fair, I suppose, that she considers me her personal dog nurse.

So who is it, down on all fours, trying to coax a mushy mash of Minute Rice and chicken broth into her gullet when she has a stomach virus? Me. Who is it trying to pry open her jaws—"Boys, go get me the crowbar"—to give her a particularly vile pill? Me. Who is it rubbing Otomax into her inflamed and infected ears, as she tries to solicit a DNA sample with her teeth? Me.

There really is nothing quite like the slapstick routine of trying to give a pill to a dog who doesn't want said pill.

We went through the typical pill rituals with Bijou. That first pill is the easiest, isn't it? It harks back to those carefree puppy days when your dog believed that every item offered from your hand was some sublime human delicacy.

Bijou wolfed down that first pill as if it were a Cheez Doodle, but followed it with her baleful poodle stare. The next time, the pill went in and came right back out, pinging to the linoleum.

She looks at the pill, then looks at us, as if to say, "Let the games begin, *mes amis*."

I pick up the pill: "Here, Bijou, want a treat?"

She sniffs at the pill: "You're kidding, right?"

I bring the pill closer to her mouth, which firmly shuts into a cute little poodle pout.

She looks at me: "Don't even think about it, buster."

I press the pill to her clenched lips—"Oh, come on, Bijou"—defeat already tainting my voice.

That elicits the upward snout pose, nose pointing toward

the ceiling in fine balletic form, mouth set into a "You'll never take me alive, coppers" grimace.

So, there we are, once again (sigh) mano a doggo, me on my knees both figuratively and literally, and Deb and the boys planted about the kitchen bleachers, laughing. And I suddenly realize that my role as paramount leader of this household is quickly slipping away at the whim of a stubborn poodle.

"Drew," I command, "get the peanut butter."

I bury Bijou's pill in half a teaspoon of PB, get back on my knees, and extend the compromise toward Her Highness as if it were a scepter, fully realizing that I am now negotiating with my dog, and not from a position of power.

Her Weaselness sniffs—her wary eyes still on me—then takes a couple tentative licks—*Where's my royal food taster?*—then commits, gulping down the peanut butter, pill and all.

The Peanut Butter Defense worked for all of a week. With the skill and savvy of a safecracker, she learned to artfully lick around the pill, leaving it forlorn on the spoon. Or, once pill and PB were in her mouth, she worked her jaws as if they were a washing-machine agitator. Peanut butter down her throat, pill on the floor, Bijou off for a nap in the sun or a heavy date with a very dirty sock.

We soon graduated to cheese slices—Kraft Singles are still known as "dog cheese" in our house—and finally to minipepperonis. Bijou is twelve years old as I write. I believe we know who won that particular battle.

The first week we had Bijou we were all outside on a sunny Sunday morning, the puppy frolicking about, kind of raccoon-like, a broad boyish smile on Owen's face as he played with *his* dog.

Then, Owen: "Bijou's choking! Bijou's choking!"

We quickly determined that she had swallowed a wood chip that we couldn't free with our fingers.

After a frantic call to the vet, we were told to gently perform the dog equivalent of the Heimlich maneuver. But not too hard, or we'd end up breaking puppy bones.

Doing the Heimlich on your new puppy simply isn't one of those situations you expect in life.

"Is she going to be all right, Dad?" Owen asked. "Is she going to be OK?"

One careful push, and the wood chip came flying out.

Bijou has had any number of medical adventures. She has epileptic seizures, has had a dog flu a couple times that we thought might kill her, and has hurt her back so badly that we thought she was paralyzed.

And the one thing that I've learned from all this is that,

to paraphrase those deep soul singers Sam and Dave, when something is wrong with my dog, there's something wrong with me.

I can't stand it when Bijou is seriously ill or in pain. When we humans are sick, we understand that there's a reason, a why that can be answered. But for dogs there's no understanding of why-ness. It just *is*. That's why dogs sometimes try to bite their pain away.

I'll never forget the first time that Bijou had an epileptic seizure.

She was still a puppy, less than a year old, and I walked into the kitchen and saw that she had peed and pooped all over the floor, which was totally out of character for her.

Turning to her, I started to scold—"Bijou? What's the matter . . ."—and I saw that she wasn't moving. She lay on the floor rigid, trembling and panting, as if she'd been hexed.

Her lips quivered and her eyes were zombie blank, but I sat down next to her, smoothing her back, and said: "You're a good girl, Bijou. Yeah, you're a good girl." At that moment, it seemed to me, she needed my presence more than anything else.

As I've said, dogs teach us the simple power of presence. So often, we—dogs and humans—just want to be near each other, need the presence of another heartbeat.

So when Bijou has a seizure I sit with her until it passes, whispering to her, petting her. I don't even know whether she knows I'm there. But it's the least I can do, the right thing to do.

When the seizure ends—sometimes after fifteen minutes, sometimes half an hour—after the demon that possessed her has fled, Bijou wobbles to her feet, stumbles to her water bowl and takes a good deep drink.

Then Bijou and I take a long, slow walk as she reacquaints herself with this world.

Being Bijou's errand boy, I actually spend more time at the vet's office than she does, as I pick up her prescriptions. And that suits Bijou just fine, because at the vet's all of Bijou de Minuit's regal airs dissolve, fizz, and shrivel like the Wicked Witch of the West at the end of *The Wizard of Oz*.

Whether it's for a checkup or an ear infection—Dr. Nancy Katz presiding—Bijou loses her poodle bravado. Once we walk through the door and settle in, she's beside herself. She crawls into my lap—and Bijou is no lap dog—burrows into my neck and *whines*.

"It's OK, girl."

. . . and *whines* . . .

"It's OK, girl."

. . . and *whines* . . .

She is only briefly mollified when Dr. Katz's gentle and beatific yellow Lab/golden retriever mix, Sarge—full name,

Sergeant Pepper Shriver—wanders over to give her a lick, a sniff, and a nudge. Once Sarge ambles off to finish his rounds, a candy-striper in fur, Bijou starts crying again.

By the time we're called into the examining room, Bijou is pretty much clinging to my neck as if she were a living, breathing poodle stole.

Bijou's seizures are wrenching—we know, though, that they're only seizures, a brief short-circuiting—but our scariest moment came the first time she hurt her back.

She jumped down from Drew's bed, as she's done thousands of times in her life, yelped, then collapsed on the floor. She couldn't move, and simply lay there, whimpering.

I scooped her into a laundry basket and rushed her to the vet. If you want to unleash a flurry of coos and clucks of sympathy, I soon found out, just walk down the street lugging a sick poodle in a laundry basket.

Bijou didn't move at all in the basket, and I was afraid that she might be paralyzed. And a paralyzed dog is no dog at all, because dogs are verbs, souls in motion.

But after a course of painkillers, by injection and by mouth, she rebounded in a couple days, started scampering after her toys, lunging at the backyard bunnies, jumping onto Drew's bed.

Our little verb was back.

Bijou de Minuit,

CANINE ZEN MASTER, SAYS:

There's nothing quite as invigorating as shoving your snout into new-fallen snow.

Double Secret Probation
Or, Harry the Frat Dog

Bijou's best buddy is Harry, a saintly golden retriever who belongs to our sons' fraternity at Dartmouth College in Hanover, New Hampshire. Drew, who once was Alpha Delta's Keeper of the Dogs (Deb and I were *so* proud), helped raise Harry from a puppy and often brought him home for holidays and school breaks. Now that Drew has graduated, Owen regularly ferries Harry to our house. We always felt that even as Drew and Owen were taking care of Harry, Harry was keeping a careful eye on them—*in doggo parentis.*

And when Harry Dawg, as he's officially known, heaves a big sigh and retires from the raucous and rowdy fraternity life, he'll be coming to live with us.

Bijou does have a few dog cousins. There's Toby (short for Toblerone), an Entlebucher ("little mountain dog") who shrieks joyous murder when he greets you; Tumble, a boisterous ball of fluff 'n' stuff who lives near Cleveland; and

Molly, a slobbery boxer who's all legs and as clumsy as a baby deer.

But Harry is Bijou's soul brother, and a good and calming influence on her.

Where Bijou is as high-strung as a diva on uppers, Harry is as mellow and down to earth as Willie Nelson. Where Bijou is a bundle of eccentricities that could make her an honorary citizen of Britain, with Harry, what you see is what you get. Where Bijou broods like Hamlet, Harry is as jovial and friendly as Falstaff.

Harry is also responsible. He gladly helped raise his canine fraternity brothers Jake, a Bernese mountain dog, and Vic, another golden retriever.

Maybe Harry is so low-key because he was raised at Alpha Delta, which was the inspiration for the movie *Animal House*. (In case you're wondering, while Harry is encouraged to hang out and even get a bit wild, he's forbidden to guzzle any beer and is not allowed to play any drinking games.) Harry and his canine kin (not to mention the occasional ferret or piranha) help put the "animal" in "Animal House."

But when Harry visits us there are no fraternity hijinks, no doggie versions of John Belushi blowouts. In fact, he's a perfect and courtly gentleman—though he always poops within five minutes of arriving, just to let the neighborhood know that he's back in town.

He greets us with his paws on our shoulders—shall we

waltz?—and a sloppy swipe of the face with his tongue, and always gives Bijou a friendly nudge with his pink nose. Bijou sometimes even deigns to curl up next to Harry and fall soundly asleep.

Harry has also taught us some valuable lessons, and we look forward to the others that he'll teach us once he moves in for good. He understands that no matter where you go you need to relax and make yourself at home; has let us know that any bed is also just the right size for two adults and a golden retriever; and that you should always bark at lions, even in suburban New Jersey: Two gaudy stone lions guard the walk of a house up the street, and when he sees them they never fail to trip some primal trigger in Harry and set him off. Wolf knowledge runs deep and dies hard.

Bijou de Minuit,

CANINE ZEN MASTER, SAYS:

Wag your tail and smile

at children

and old ladies.

Silence of the Jumble Cookies

Jumble cookies are a family favorite; a sweet, dense mixture of nuts, raisins, and chocolate chips. It's the kind of baking that Bijou prefers, because there's a good chance that some scrumptious chunk will plunk to the floor—and what falls on the floor (or in the dirt at the cave), since time immemorial, belongs to the dog. That's why Bijou sits patiently in the kitchen when Deb cooks or bakes.

Here's the recipe for jumble cookies, from Deb's files:

¾ cup pecan halves
¾ cup unblanched whole almonds
1½ cups semisweet chocolate chips
1½ cups raisins
8 tablespoons (¼ pound) unsalted butter
½ cup sugar
¼ cup light brown sugar

1 egg
¾ teaspoon vanilla
1 cup and 2 tablespoons flour
1 teaspoon baking soda
¼ teaspoon salt

Chop the nuts into coarse pieces. Stir in a large bowl with the chocolate chips and raisins.

Soften butter and cream with both sugars until light and fluffy. Beat in egg and vanilla until blended.

In small bowl, sift flour, baking soda, and salt, then whisk to mix evenly. On low speed, beat flour mixture into butter mixture, then mix in nut mixture by hand.

Drop by the tablespoonful onto baking sheets, one and a half inches apart. Bake 12 to 15 minutes at 375 degrees until golden brown and barely soft. Cool for a few minutes on sheets. When firm enough to lift, transfer to wire rack to cool completely.

What makes the recipe even more intriguing and complicated is when you mix in a nosy miniature poodle.

Deb and I were hosting a going-away party for one of her teaching colleagues: the India pale ales, stouts, and porters were chilling on the deck, sandwiches and salads waited on the dining-room table, and the cheese was sweating. We'd set snacks on a low table in the living room—peanuts and chips, bowls of M&Ms, a veggie platter, a couple dozen jumble cookies.

As Deb made one more obsessive-compulsive sweep through the house—that's an observation, not a criticism—I fretted over what music best suited this party. Muddy Waters and Howlin' Wolf? Waylon and Willie? Early Elvis, Carl Perkins, Jerry Lee Lewis, and those other rugged rockabilly rioters on Sun Records? I finally settled on *Beg, Scream, and Shout! The Big Ol' Box of 60s Soul.*

Neither one of us heard Bijou tiptoe into the living room.

"Mooooooom! Bijou's eating the cooooookies!"

We scrambled into the living room. It's funny how, when given a choice between a platter of celery, carrots, and radishes and a platter of cookies, a dog will always go for the cookies.

"Bijou!"

She gave us the classic sideways dog look—"Who? Me?"—her black snout encrusted in brown cookie crumbs, her tail tremoring in approval at Deb's baking.

"Bijou!"

Every single jumble cookie was gone, devoured by Her Dogness. There were more crumbs on her muzzle than there were on the platter.

"Bijou!"

She stared up at us with her "I'm-a-good-girl-right?" look. And all we could do was laugh.

"Bijou!"

For the record, not one celery stick had been touched. And, amazingly, Bijou didn't get sick. We ordered her upstairs, where she contentedly flopped onto Drew's bed and slept the deep and full sleep of gluttons.

"Good girl!"

Bijou de Minuit,

CANINE ZEN MASTER, SAYS:

Funky toes taste even better

than funky socks.

Dog Time, Cancer Time

Bijou, like all dogs, runs on primal time. She isn't constantly barking on her cell and doesn't stay up late to catch Conan or Letterman. She eats when she's hungry, drinks when she's dry, and naps when she's sleepy. The absolute, very best moment is the one that she's inhabiting *right now*—whether stalking a bunny, shredding a sock, or snoring away in a swatch of sunlight. And during and after cancer, I also came to understand that the very best moment is *right now*.

Cancer, like any dog, insists on its own time, also runs on primal time. If you try to defy it, it can break you, physically and spiritually. So, as I coped with prostate cancer, I took some cues from Bijou. I ate when I was hungry, drank when I was dry, and napped when I was sleepy.

Cancer doesn't know from deadlines and BlackBerries, from Twittering and overnight delivery. It is analog and organic in a digital world. If you have a Type A personality, you will need to adjust to Type C—for cancer. (Or, even better, Type D for dog.)

Each phase of the disease—diagnosis, surgery, radiation and other treatment—carries its own distinct sense of stepping outside traditional time, its own bitter flavor of dislocation.

I went on Cancer Standard Time the moment I learned, at age fifty, that I had prostate cancer. I'd had a biopsy three days before, and I thought I fully understood that the odds were fifty-fifty that I might have the disease. Yet, I realize now, I secretly believed that I couldn't possibly have cancer. *That* only happened to other people.

In the instant that I found out, I felt stuck in time—What? What? What?—like a scratched CD skipping and stuttering in the player. I wondered whether I had heard wrong.

I chose to have my prostate removed, and the three months between the diagnosis and the radical open prostatectomy were a blur. I was swept up in a whirlwind of tests and scans, treatment decisions and negotiations with my insurer. (They were hostage negotiations, with me as the hostage.) Those days hurtled forward, caught in the gravitational pull of surgery.

In the hospital, time held no meaning. Once I entered that always unsettling time machine of anesthesia, and came out breathing on the other side, I inhabited each hazy post-op moment, not worrying about the past or the future. All

I knew was that I could hit the morphine drip every ten minutes, that I could nap whenever I wanted.

Those three days revolved around the cycles of doing the hospital shuffle, of having my four drains emptied, of having my blood pressure and temperature taken. I didn't quite know what day it was, and it didn't quite matter. I was alive. I trusted the date printed on page 1 of *The New York Times*.

Then life became more complicated.

Nine days after surgery, I received the results of my pathology report. I found out that my probably Stage 1 prostate cancer, which had appeared ordinary enough, was unexpectedly aggressive. It had surged through the prostate and was now classified as a Stage T3B. More treatment was needed.

I used to joke that my goal was to live to 106, making a gradual transition from writer to sage. When I was given my pathology report, I felt all those taken-for-granted decades squirming through my fingers. Age 106? Let's shoot for 60, or even 51.

But before I could focus on the next phases of therapy—hormone shots and radiation—I had to complete my post-op healing. You have to become healthy before more treatment can damage you again in the name of curing you.

But healing, too, comes in its own time. No matter how hard you push—and pushing isn't necessarily bad—you have to understand that the cancer and its treatment will push back.

I spent seven weeks recuperating from surgery that summer, and time once again bent in weird ways. It was the first summer I hadn't worked since I was fourteen, and I luxuriated in the languors of childhood: comic books and rhythm 'n' blues, walks and spontaneous naps, and, of course, my loyal pooch.

As I convalesced, there was a fairy-tale sense of being outside of time. I half expected to see vines and creepers swaddling my house, as if I were some kind of Sleeping Beauty with a buzz cut. The world's quaint concerns weren't my concerns. Obama? McCain? Palin? Oh, if you insist.

That was partly why returning to work that August was so jarring. On the streets of Manhattan I had lost a couple of steps. I felt myself in sharp relief to the frenzy of zoom and zip that characterizes New York. Whenever I tried to push ahead physically, the cancer, the healing, the treatment pushed back, reminding me that, after all, I was still a patient.

It was like a physics problem: If the world accelerates, but cancer makes you decelerate, where does that leave you?

Radiation treatment posed that question even more profoundly. Radiation is exhausting, and I felt as if I had been nudged into an alternate timeline. I kept working, kept up some semblance of a social life. But I also seemed to fall behind. I had somehow traveled outside time, and my frame of mind felt gray and snowy, like some Eastern bloc city of the 1950s.

With Bijou as an example, though, I understood that living

in the moment was crucial. But what if you can't grasp the moment? What if you feel as if you're living in no-moment? I sometimes felt like one of those forlorn characters in old-time songs who moan, "Dark hollows will be my home."

But there's nothing like a dog to snap you back to the moment. Bijou's cold nose nudging my hand or her warm tongue licking my foot would bring me back to this world, bring me back to myself, like the prince who kisses Sleeping Beauty to bring her back to the here and now.

Bijou de Minuit,

CANINE ZEN MASTER, SAYS:

When it comes to taking pills,

always hold out for the

pepperoni wrap.

The Secret Lives of Dogs

Most dogs are as straightforward as a guy who's owned a hardware store in Omaha, Nebraska, for fifty years. What you see is what you get.

But other dogs are more mysterious. They hover at doors and windows as if awaiting word from some canine cabal, they hear things that you can't hear, and you always wonder just what keeps them at the computer for so long.

Bijou falls into this latter category.

I readily admit that I sometimes ponder Bijou's secret life, wonder about her beyond-the-house alter ego. Given her pedigree and her persnickety combination of intelligence and insolence, I fancy her slipping into her little black dress and beret after midnight and stealing into town.

Once there, I see her smoking Gauloises and sipping pooch espressos and cappuccinos with the other members of the local dogerati—the pugs and the Boston terriers, the Ibizans and the always unruly Australian border collies—as they discuss Sartre, Beckett, and universal health care for dogs.

We have never actually caught Bijou at this, but we still have our suspicions. Maybe it's because we paper-trained her with copies of *Le Monde. C'est la vie.*

Probably the most disconcerting thing Bijou does is the thousand-yard dog stare. This isn't to be confused with the aforementioned intense dog stare.

The thousand-yard stare generally involves Bijou sitting at attention and either scrutinizing a wall or gazing into space.

"Bijou?"

She doesn't move.

When Bijou enters this state she's eerily reminiscent of any number of 1950s science fiction movies in which crafty and malicious aliens steal the bodies and souls of oblivious earthlings—*Invasion of the Dog-Snatchers*, anyone?

"Bijou?"

It's as if she's receiving highly secret instructions from someone somewhere beyond the Twilight Zone: Nostradamus? The CIA? Voldemort?

"Bijou?"

Then, with a rattly shake of her head (and, perhaps, a sly glance at whoever's watching), it's over. She ambles off for a drink, a snack, and another nap—probably pondering which dress to wear that night.

Bijou de Minuit,

CANINE ZEN MASTER, SAYS:

Before you eat, nap, and poop, circle around looking for snakes, wolverines, and wildcats—especially wildcats.

Those Darned Socks
Or, Kill the Bunny

Pity the poor stray sock, separated from the paired herds safely tucked away in dresser drawers. Whether clean dress sock or funky mud-encrusted jock sock, it belongs to Bijou.

Spotting her prey—perhaps lured by its rank soccer-sweat reek—Bijou crouches, nose-to-floor, head lower than her rear end, tail quivering. Slap four tires on her and she'd look like a mini-Corvette.

Creeping closer to the clueless sock—*ah, game-used Adidas*—her head moves side to side, on the lookout for other potential hose-ivores (or maybe to make sure that she has an audience).

Then she *pounces*.

The sock is in her mouth. Bijou snarls and growls—tail still fluttering in joy—and snaps her head back and forth as if breaking the neck of a rabbit or a possum or a particularly feisty Cheez Doodle.

"Kill the bunny, Bijou! Go ahead, kill the bunny!"

Her growls grow more fierce, her head snaps more sharply. The sock goes limp and damp and, finally, she drops it.

She gives it one more flip with her nose—making sure it's dead, I suppose—then stalks off in pursuit of bigger game. A pair of boxers, maybe, or a bra, or even better, a platter of jumble cookies.

While Bijou delights in humiliating a lonely and stinky sock, what she likes even better is a full basket of clean laundry fresh out of the dryer.

There's nothing quite like curling up like a cat—please don't let Loki know about this—for a nap on a warm pile of cotton towels.

Bijou de Minuit,

CANINE ZEN MASTER, SAYS:

Only give your paw if there's a treat

in the other hand.

Good Morning!
Good Morning!

As is often the case with young men—especially if they've been up till three in the morning the previous night—our sons like to sleep late on the weekends when they're home. In fact, they'd sleep till two in the afternoon, if we let them.

But Bijou is an effective, if soppy, alarm clock.

"Want to go get Drew, Bijou? Want to get Drew?"

She sits outside Drew's bedroom door, her body trembling, tail pulsing.

"Want to get Drew?"

She's about jumping out of her fur by the time I open his door. "Get him, Bijou! Go get him!"

Like some mini-ninja Bijou hurtles into the room, bounds onto the bed, pounces on Drew's chest, and starts licking the sleep from her boy's face.

"Ohhhh, Bijou," Drew groans as she keeps at him, as if she's tussling with a fellow puppy from her litter.

Once she's persuaded that Drew's awake, Bijou jumps down, then waits outside Owen's door.

"Want to get Owen, Bijou? Want to get Owen?"

🐾

Morning, of course, means breakfast—not that Bijou hasn't already been peed, pilled, and fed—and another startling peek at Cheerios lust.

Cheerios are Bijou's absolute favorite food in the world. She likes them all: original, honey-nut, frosted, multigrain—do you remember the days when cold cereal didn't take up an entire supermarket aisle?—but the ones that make her caterwaul and levitate in doggish joy are Apple-Cinnamon Cheerios.

Purina Dog Chow? You've got to be kidding, right? Dog chow gets you through the day. But Cheerios are the oats of transcendence.

Once she hears the shake, rattle, and crinkle of a cereal box, Bijou magically appears in the kitchen, sitting at attention, gearing up the intense dog stare. If I just stare hard enough . . . If I just stare hard enough . . . If I just stare hard enough . . .

Now, her ache for Cheerios could just be her way of reminding us that the cereal consists of heart-healthy oats that help lower cholesterol. She *is* a smart dog, after all. But I think it's just because they taste really, really good.

Before I pour myself a bowl, I shake a few Cheerios into

my hand and drop them in front of Bijou. It never hurts to appease the dog gods before you start the day.

As I eat, Bijou quietly sits. Sure, she's already gotten her apple-cinnamon graft, but you never know when someone's going to spill. And, as a dog, it's your duty and responsibility to be ready. It's in the handbook. And, of course, there's Owen, who's been known to slyly slip Bijou the occasional handoff from the table.

One morning Bijou's persistence paid off in a big way and she achieved Cheerios nirvana. We call it the Big Spill.

I was opening a new box of Apple-Cinnamon Cheerios, mangling and shredding the box top in the process—have you noticed that cereal boxes (and grocery bags) are nowhere near as sturdy as they used to be? When I popped open the wax-paper pouch my hand slipped, the box tumbled, and a deluge of Cheerios rained on the linoleum, scattering and clattering.

Bijou's eyes glittered and glowed—*ahhh*, the prophecies were true.

The house rule, as I've said, is that whatever falls on the floor belongs to Bijou, which generally means the occasional butterscotch morsel or macaroni elbow or scrap of hamburger. But half a box of Cheerios? That was almost a miracle in Bijou's eyes.

In no rush, Bijou methodically marched from one end of the kitchen to the other, snarfing up the Big Spill. Then she obsessively performed a perimeter sweep.

I was so proud. My dog, the vacuum cleaner.

Bijou de Minuit,

CANINE ZEN MASTER, SAYS:

Always leave a little food
in your bowl. Who knows when
the next meal's coming.

Shrinking the World to the Size of a Dog

In the wake of having cancer, more than ever I wanted to stay home—wanted to shrink the world to the couple of rooms in my house where I was most comfortable. Wanted to shrink the world to the size of Bijou.

I declined requests for my time, and the social whirl was less compelling than it had been. To me, a perfect evening often meant stretching out in the den and vanishing into a good novel or compact disc. I envied Bijou, snoring away on her bed, and her twenty-plus hours of downtime each day.

As I underwent treatment for my cancer, my retreat was something I needed to do. It was part of the healing process, of coming to grips with my new vulnerability. I have to admit that the impulse became more dangerous as I struggled with post-treatment depression, felt like a book coming loose from its binding. It's a thin line between the necessary womb of healing and cutting yourself off from the world.

Even so, I wanted to nest. I was doing well physically—my blood tests couldn't have been better and I regularly took five-mile walks—but my spirit was still convalescing. I craved homely days built around writing, reading, and walking, and time spent with family, friends and, of course, Bijou.

I fully believe in the paradox that if you make your world small enough, it can become the universe. And right then, my town—and Bijou—was enough of the world for me.

I grew up in northern New England, and I was feeding my inner Yankee hermit who would like nothing better than to live in a cabin a couple miles down a pocked logging road with a couple loyal hounds. I suppose that I bend to this inclination naturally. I come from a long and leathery line of ornery, horn-handed men who burned their lonesome days wrestling with snapping turtles, squinting at pickerel, junking cars, and picking the dump.

I preferred my coffee (and ale) dark, bold, and bitter as I recovered, but I took pleasure in the most gentle rhythms of daily life: meeting a crony for breakfast, getting a haircut, walking Bijou. Solitude was an agreeable pal.

I was still reinterpreting myself in the face of cancer, and that takes time and quiet. It can't be rushed, and I couldn't do it successfully if I was caught up in our huckster culture's unrelenting ruckus.

And I still don't want to be among tens of thousands of people shrilling and shrieking at a football game or a Springsteen concert at Giants Stadium. An hour of hushed conversation at Starbucks or a few seconds spent stroking your dog's paws is more than enough, is the true DNA of our finite lives.

Through all of this I started simplifying my life, both consciously and subconsciously, as if trying to flense myself to something elemental.

I discovered the deep joy of culling my possessions, rather than being possessed by them. It thrills me to dispense with moldering piles of crispy paperbacks, rickety stacks of compact discs, and ragged flannel shirts that look as if they once belonged to Kurt Cobain. I obsessively kill old e-mail messages as if they were cancer cells.

When Owen took our second car to college, I was glad it was gone. The more errands I do on foot, the better, because, like Bijou, I always feel most like myself when I'm out and about.

Walking is the family station wagon in the world of exercise, about as cool as great-grandma doing the Electric Slide at her favorite Club Med resort. There's no gear except for a practical pair of shoes, no need for a chiseled coach or trainer and Under Armour is optional. You want cool? Try mountain-biking or in-line skating or climbing K2.

But as much as I like to run or ride my Schwinn, it's walking—plain old dowdy walking—that was a crucial part of my recovery. From shuffling the hospital hallways, to creeping through my neighborhood, to roving around town, walking has been my physical constant during and after cancer. And Bijou was often there, too, snuffling along beside me.

I took raw pleasure in the simple physicality of walking after I had surgery. It was a way to measure myself—my endurance, my incontinence, the tightness of my abdominal scar. As that scar relaxed its grip on my gut, I knew I was getting better.

In those first weeks after surgery I felt as if I were impersonating those drawings that chart the progress of man, as I lurched from *Homo hunched-overus* to *Homo erectus* to *Homo sapiens*.

After being cooped up in the hospital and in my sickbed, there was an exquisite sense of freedom, a joy in being out and about. I got to know myself better, too—body and soul. For me, walking is a way of thinking, of scrutinizing worlds both exterior and interior. The slowness and noticing that comes with a stroll suits the recovering patient well.

In the face of cancer, of any serious disease, movement is defiance. Movement affirms that we are still alive and walking, if not necessarily kicking. A glaze of sweat lubricates the body, keeps it from seizing up the way oil and grease keep a car going. A light sweat, too, is a kind of balm.

Movement thumbs its nose at the notion that patients must be solitary, stationary, dependent. Walking, for me, has worked against the sometimes overwhelming urge to shrink my world to the secret garden of my den, where I can hide and brood amid the books and the CDs and my own dark thoughts.

There are the practical physical benefits, too, that come with walking: the promise of lower blood pressure and heart rate, better sleep, and mental sharpness. Walking helps scour the sludge, physical and mental, from the body.

More specifically, walking helped me battle the weight gain caused by hormone therapy, and blunt, just a bit, the fatigue caused by radiation. It also taught me to start trusting my mutinous body again.

I got to know my town better, too, became a familiar face in neighborhoods miles from home. I stumbled upon the unexpected, small pools of pleasant shock, that felt inexplicably healing to me: train tracks vanishing both east and west at sundown, a sluggish brook packed with gloom and murk and the reek of leafy decay, the new arrivals in the display window of Watchung Booksellers, my local bookstore.

My favorite time to walk was at dusk, to the sounds of the crazed cicadas and crickets. I spotted fawns grazing on the soccer field, and rabbits nibbling in the shadows. I stayed out late enough to watch porch lights ease on, and the fireflies second that notion.

During that time I also gorged on young adult fantasy novels: books chockablock with magic and mystery by Neil Gaiman and Jonathan Stroud, J. K. Rowling and Rick Riordan, Ursula K. Le Guin and Cornelia Funke.

I felt as if I were questing after my core boyhood innocence, trying to conjure the dreamy kid who spent hour upon hour on the summer porch writing and reading and drawing. I miss the boy I was (with Tiny at my heels)—everyone called me Andy in that time and place—who couldn't imagine having cancer or doing the zombie shuffle through the shadowland of depression.

As I took the reading cure in my den—snubbing (with great relish) the insistent ring of the telephone—I realized that I was trying to re-create that long-ago porch, trying to make my world manageable enough to wrap it about myself and Bijou like a prayer shawl.

Bijou de Minuit,

CANINE ZEN MASTER, SAYS:

The well-placed snarl and snap

keep everyone honest.

Ready, Set, Go!

Dogs are verbs. When you live in the eternal present, there's no choice. Socrates said the unexamined life isn't worth living. When you're a dog, the inactive life isn't worth living.

Bijou profoundly and instinctively knows this.

She is a bunny-lunging, sock-shredding, Cheerio-munching, carcass-snuffling, wind-sniffing (but not butt-sniffing), sun-worshipping mystery.

And she has the dog basics down pat. She eats, drinks, and humps. She barks and howls, whines and growls, snarls and sniffs.

She begs, borrows, and steals . . . she noses ears, licks her paws (and stray toes), and chases her tail . . . she dances and fetches, nuzzles and snuggles, snorts and sighs.

Even when she sleeps, even when she naps, Bijou snores, twitches, and lets go with random yips. But I wouldn't expect anything less from our fuzzy little verb.

And as I recovered from treatment for my cancer, I appreciated her verbness even more. My verbs had been throttled back: sleeping, and sleeping some more, reading and listening to music, sighing into my rocking chair, and scuffing to the bathroom.

Watching Bijou caper through her daily paces made me smile—as if I were siphoning a bit of her abundant energy—and made me look forward to the day when I could once again take her for a walk, when we could be verbs together.

Bijou has always been ready to serve up a jolt of her abundant canine energy. When I used to work nights, getting home at one or two in the morning, she'd shrug herself awake and bound into the kitchen. I'd drink a beer, and we'd share a bag of Cheez Doodles, the bright orange cheese dust powdering her whiskers. Then we'd ramble outside, the neighborhood buttoned up and sound asleep. It was so quiet that I could hear Bijou's feet padding on the pavement, hear her urine sizzle into the dirt.

And as I struggled with post-cancer depression, Bijou's presence never failed to slice through the fog that weighed me down. Sure, therapy, Zoloft, and Wellbutrin helped me recover, let me become myself again, but regular doses of Bijou de Minuit's sheer dogginess also helped me become whole again.

There's nothing like a brisk shock of doggie energy to help you snap out of it.

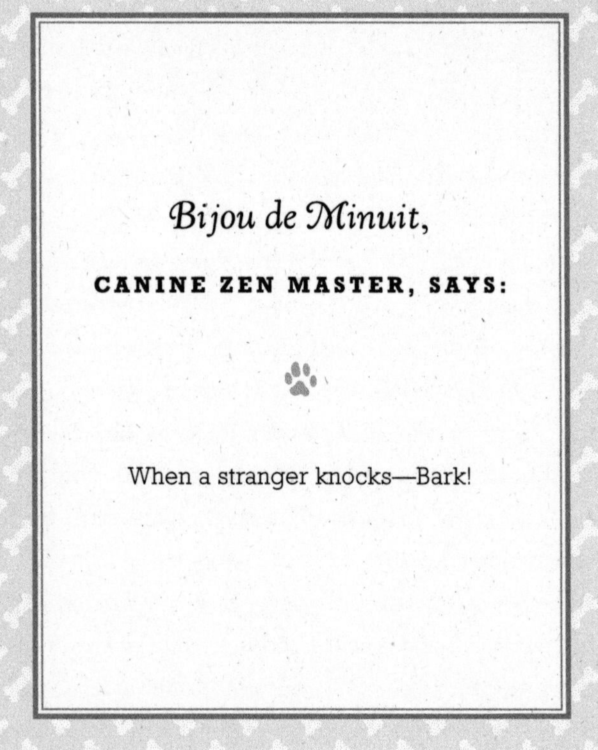

Bijou de Minuit,

CANINE ZEN MASTER, SAYS:

When a stranger knocks—Bark!

Your Beds Are My Beds, All of Them

Like that fairy-tale sneak Goldilocks, Bijou is forever in search of the perfect bed.

It's no great secret that dogs like to sleep. In fact, by my calculations, Bijou is awake exactly 27 minutes 43 seconds a day, which lets her fit in two meals, the requisite walks, and a couple romps with her little rubber soccer ball.

Let Lassie and Benji squander their lives on high adventure. Bijou wants to sleep.

So, when you're sleeping 23 hours 32 minutes 17 seconds a day, you need some variety in your sleeping arrangements. Being an absolute sun dog, Bijou's ideal is to melt into a puddle of sunlight on Drew's bed, where the window faces south and overlooks the backyard and driveway. This is her favorite post from which to perform her duties as house sentinel.

As she saunters from sleeping station to sleeping station, like a night watchman making his rounds, Bijou is never averse to tossing a couple of pillows with her dainty snout before tucking in for a snooze.

After sunlight, Bijou's most important requirement is elevation. Like mountain goats, army generals, and messiahs, she seeks the high ground: the back of the living-room couch, the upstairs hall, Drew's bed.

You can't keep an eye on the neighborhood and bark your tail off if you can't see what's going on.

Then there are those arctic winter nights when Bijou decides that it's time to wriggle under the covers, her winter coat not quite plush enough to make her feel toasty.

She'll jump on the bed, always on Deb's side, and eventually migrate between us, warm and snug, her head on a pillow, ready for a long winter's nap.

Bijou de Minuit,

CANINE ZEN MASTER, SAYS:

Walking the dog is more calming than

a glass of fine cabernet.

That Dirty Old Egg-Sucking Dog

Whether city mutt, suburban pooch, or country hound, our dogs embody a profound lust for the deep past and a quest for solace. And a classic country song does the same thing.

I was raised in the piney sticks of the North Country. When I was born, in 1957, my hometown of Kingston, New Hampshire (Pop. 900), had more cows than people. I grew up among eight-fingered loggers and junkyard alchemists, dirt farmers and shade-tree mechanics. And they were always aching for a good country song that they could disappear into for a few minutes—tunes by singers like Merle Haggard and Buck Owens, Patsy Cline and Loretta Lynn. And, too, they were always searching for just the right dog with whom they could share their loneliness and a Pabst Blue Ribbon beer or three.

There's something pure and primal in most of us that longs for the old homeplace—a homeplace that might not be possible to articulate but that still haunts us—and it's there in our dogs, too. Bijou and I aren't so far removed from our ancestors who would have killed for a warm, dry cave and a fierce fire to ward off the cold and the demons of the night.

Bijou might be a total suburbanista, but she still knows how to yowl and howl, will still stand on point, is still grateful for a squirrel carcass. She loves Apple-Cinnamon Cheerios, but there's a part of her that's still feral, still country wild. And I agree wholeheartedly with Ms. Lynn, who once sang, When you're looking at me, you're looking at country.

There's a long and venerable tradition of country songs that have dogs coursing and chorusing through them, tunes like "Old Shep" by Red Foley, "Move It on Over" by Hank Williams, "I'm on My Way Back to the Old Home" by Bill Monroe, and (cover your ears, Bijou) "Dirty Old Egg-Sucking Dog" by Johnny Cash.

These canine tunes sing me back home, and suddenly I'm bushwhacking through the woods with Tiny, or Uncle Junior is wrestling in the dooryard with his mutt, Spike, or some hound dog is hanging his head out the window of some old Ford pickup—ears whipping back in the wind—as the truck groans and jounces down the power-line road.

It was Grammy Jennings who taught me to love a good dog *and* a good country song. Her life itself was a country song. She was one hellion of an orphan who kept running away from the orphanage and had tuberculosis when she was a young woman (just like Jimmie Rodgers, the father of country music, in "T.B. Blues"). Stray dogs *and* stray men would wander into her dooryard because they knew they could get a good meal, a kind word, and a scratch behind the ears.

Grammy never had much money and found herself on relief more than once in her life. Her years were a sorry succession of tarpaper shacks, rickety rent houses, and rust-rabid trailers. But she always had room for a few animals: hamsters and guinea pigs, cats and white mice and, especially, dogs—though I could've done without the house adder that lived under the steps of one of her wild hovels.

Being only four foot ten herself, Grammy especially loved the runt of any litter, dog or cat. She'd warm them next to the woodstove as if they were biscuits, smear their scrawny and heaving chests with Vicks VapoRub, and feed them milk through an eyedropper. It was her small way of trying to heal this flawed world. And as she cared for her furry flock, she took solace in songs that spoke of heartache and broken whiskey promises, of truck-driving daredevils and the lonesome sigh and moan of that midnight train, and in songs, of course, about dogs.

Red Foley's "Old Shep"—"When I was a boy and Old Shep was a pup . . ."—is a tearjerker, a sentimental template for any sad dog tale that you've ever heard. (By the way, when Elvis Presley was ten years old, he sang "Old Shep" before a few hundred people in a talent show at the Mississippi-Alabama Fair and Dairy Show in Tupelo. At that point in his career, teenage girls were not sobbing, wailing, and swooning when he sang.)

In "Move It on Over," Hank Williams gleefully tells the tale of a guy who's ticked off his woman and has been banished to a literal doghouse, while in "I'm on the Way to the Old Home," a song of exquisite longing, Bill Monroe harks back to the idyllic days when he used to listen to the foxhounds bay at dusk back in the old Kentucky hills.

But it's Johnny Cash's "Dirty Old Egg-Sucking Dog" that makes me think most about Bijou, New Hampshire, and my grandmother. (This song, by the way, is on *Johnny Cash at Folsom Prison*, which was Grammy Jennings's favorite record album.) Cash's beast is the opposite of the saintly Shep. He's shaggy and ugly, keeps killing the chickens, and "eats like a hog." Cash threatens to kill the old reprobate, but his laughter as he sings tells us that he never, ever would.

My Bijou is shaggy and wart-mottled, keeps killing socks and jumble cookies, and also "eats like a hog." But dogs teach us to love them, despite their faults, even as they stick with us, despite our own.

Bijou de Minuit,

CANINE ZEN MASTER, SAYS:

If your tail offends you,

chase it.

Bijou in Autumn

I was born in October and autumn is my favorite season. I'm always on the lookout for that certain August night when the midnight breeze shifts just a bit, the season turns, and I suddenly smell September in the air, pleasant and bitter.

I look forward to the low and slow mourning of the late crickets, and the frenzied honeybees lured by the sweet fizz of Cokes and beers. The crisp copper light sharpens the woods and fields, and at dusk the old oaks stand as dark and stark as ancient kings. And, of course, the leaves burst into flame, as incandescent as dragon scales, before crabbing into brown and arthritic fists. Soon, the thinnest skin of ice will membrane the frog ponds, and some night after an early owl-light it will be spitting snow.

Bijou looks forward to autumn, too. She shakes off the doggie lethargy of August, her step more nimble, her tail more erect. Instead of conserving energy and panting at her spot at the top of the stairs, she roams the house for those refreshing pools of fall sunlight. She sniffs the wind—more full-bodied now—with complete interest. Nothing pleases her more than to squat on a pile of belly-scratching leaves to pee, and not one crinkly leaf skitters by that she doesn't think is a potato chip.

As I write, though, Bijou herself is in autumn now.

She sighs and creaks like the oaks in a November wind, and as the trees lose their leaves, she's shedding some of her fur. Those same brittle leaves cling to her head and muzzle, King Lear–like, like an autumnal crown. And she has lost her girlish figure. Where once she spent most of her life as twenty-three pounds of svelte fury, she now weighs thirty pounds and bumbles about like a badger or a raccoon. The prednisone she takes for her pain makes her ravenous—she has even taken to scarfing up bird berries off the ground—and we see little point in denying her food in her old age. What's a dog treat or two in the face of eternity?

Even so, our Bijou is hanging on, like that last stubborn leaf that clutches at a fall maple.

For most of this book I've written about Bijou as she was, in her eternal present tense. And, years from now, that's how we'll remember her: the frisky puppy gnawing on our fingers with her needle-like milk teeth, the feisty bitch refusing to give up her dead bird, Her Highness ruling the nearest available throne of sunlight.

We won't as readily recall her shadow self.

Bijou's serious health problems began the winter after my surgery for prostate cancer, as I was finishing the radiation and hormone therapy that left me exhausted and uncertain about the future.

Even as I faced my own profound health issues, it was my dog's poor health that pierced me to the heart.

I dreaded that morning when I'd walk downstairs and . . . well, those of us who love dogs understand that all dog stories end the same way.

As I write, Bijou is literally on her last legs. Her hind quarters fly out from beneath her, her back cricks and cracks as she walks, she limps, she's speckled with those bright red warts the size of nickels, her snore is loud and labored (like a freight train chugging up some mountain grade), and she spends most of the day drowsing on her pillow-bed.

Despite all her troubles, Bijou is still game. She still groans to her feet to go outside, still barks and bickers with the neighborhood dogs, is willing to hobble around the kitchen to carouse with a rubber ball—her shrubby tail quaking in joy.

The cancer has taken its toll on me, both physically and mentally, but, following Bijou's example, I'm still game, too. I'm not as strong as I used to be, and fatigue is a constant companion. I shake my head at the boy I once was who'd lug home heavy bags of cement from Cheney's Mill and who could run ten miles without hardly thinking about it.

But I refuse to give in. I walk five miles a day, and I've lost more than twenty-five pounds of the weight I gained when I was getting injected with hormones.

And in considering myself and Bijou as we've wrestled with our aches and pains, I've come to understand that as we age our bodies become coarser, but our spirits become finer. Wisdom always arrives with a price.

In spending so much time with Bijou as I recuperated, I began to realize that our dogs, in their carefree dogginess, make us more human, force us to shed our narcissistic skins. Even when you have cancer, you can't be utterly self-involved when there's a floppy-eared mutt to be fed, walked, and belly-scratched.

And I don't know about you, but I can't help but ponder the mysteries of creation as I gaze into Bijou's eyes, or wonder why and how we chose dogs . . . and they chose us.

Dogs also tell us—especially when we're sick—of our own finitude. And partly, that's why we cry when they die, because we also know that all human-being stories end the same way, too.

These days, Bijou just might be teaching us her most profound lessons.

She sleeps later than she used to. Instead of her waking me up, I'm the one who rouses her. But she's always ready to go, always happy to see me when she hears me trot down the stairs.

As we ease outside, strolling the sidewalk, she's in no

rush. There are trees to sniff for new messages, disgusting things to lick off the sidewalk, the occasional dog buddy to bark at, and the inevitable Loki the cat with whom to share the requisite inscrutable stares.

Her legs may be weak, but she steels herself to spring up the steps. And she still watches me carefully as I get her fresh water, pour her a bowl of chow, and wrap her five pills in the mandatory mini-pepperoni.

She won't crunch into her chow, though, until I've left the room. She's still her sweet, quirky self, despite her aches and pains.

I like it at night, as I read in the den and she's dozing nearby, when she wakes, stands up, shakes off the sleep, then wobbles over to me. She brushes against me a couple times, as if making sure that I'm awake, then rests her chin on the cushion of the chair.

I scratch her pointy head and rub her lush ears as she shuts her eyes in satisfaction. Finally, she sighs in gratitude and saunters off for another nap or to see what the rest of the household is up to.

All is well with the world.

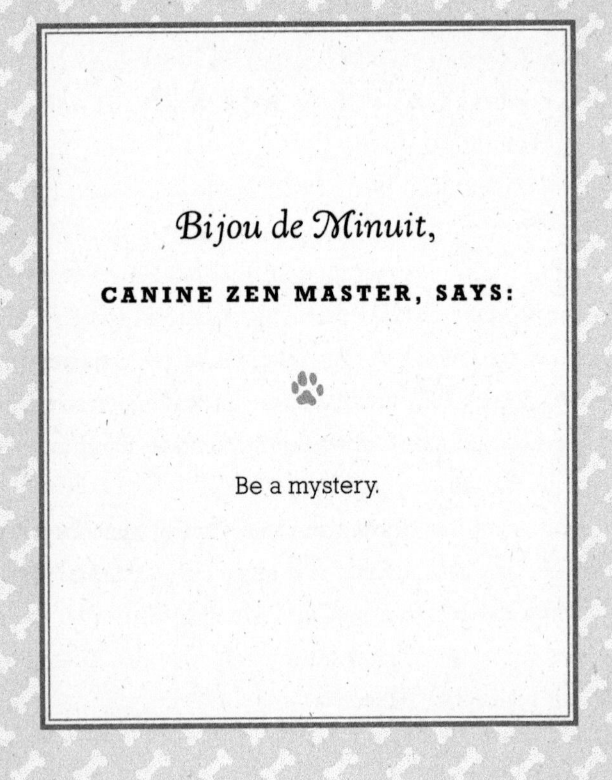

Bijou de Minuit,

CANINE ZEN MASTER, SAYS:

Be a mystery.

If There Are No Dogs in Heaven

As I get older, and especially since I learned I had cancer, I linger even longer and more lovingly over the past. But I'm not just tugged at by the satisfactions of mere nostalgia. In following those lonely and haunted dirt roads back to my hick childhood, I'm also on a quest to try to understand the adult that I've become.

And that journey down the highways of memory always dead-ends back with me standing in my crib: I'm laughing and being licked in the face by Midnight the black Lab as Dad holds her up to me, offering me my first canine communion.

What a wonderful place for consciousness to begin, with a giddy and wriggling puppy anointing me for the voyage ahead. And, in a sense, it's a perfect memory.

There's the absolute joy of the moment, of boy, puppy, and father, but it's tempered by the bittersweet knowledge that the puppy will soon be dead. This is my only memory of Midnight.

I can't tell you how often I hear dog people say: "If there are no dogs in heaven, I want to go where they go."

What is it about our dogs that gets us thinking about heaven, about matters of ultimate concern? What is it about our dogs that pierces us to the depths of our souls?

If there is a heaven, some sort of afterlife, I like to think of it as a place where we get reunited with all the good dogs that we've ever known.

I'll be baptized once again by Midnight. Twinkles will cry in delight when she sees me, and King will stop excavating his craters long enough to take me for a wild ride on his broad back. And Tiny, Bijou, Harry, and who knows how many others will all yip and howl in joy. They will all leap into my lap, knocking me over, and Emma the beagle will bay in pleasure and forgiveness.

Each one of our good dogs is a psalm, a prayer, a song of praise—on four legs and with a wagging tail. The only reason any dog turns from the good is because it has been corrupted by the evil of men.

No matter how many thousands of times it happens, it always makes me smile when Bijou or Harry or Fern up the street or even a dog I don't know raises her head toward me in expectation and devotion.

Dogs seek our giving hands in the same way that flowers seek the sun.

As I write, Bijou is still hanging in there, snoring and

snoozing, begging for baguette crumbs and Cheerios, grimacing up and down the steps, still barking in the bark club—still teaching all of us to be game, even on our last legs.

Just to touch our dogs is enough to calm us down, enough to soothe us.

As I scratch the knot of curls atop Bijou's head, she sighs, shuts her eyes, and collapses to the floor. And I smile and shut my eyes in pleasure, too, as my fingers work her stiff curls.

The insides of her ears are pale and soft and irresistible, like the inside of an abalone shell, while the pads of her feet are as smooth as the leather of a well-worn baseball glove—this fuzzy miracle dozing next to me.

I'm hanging in there, too, my cancer in remission, looking ahead to the weddings of my sons, to grandchildren and, of course, to the dogs I'll love that I haven't even met yet. The dogs we haven't yet brought into our home, into our lives.

One of the gateways to true adulthood is when we finally understand that even as we live, we are moving toward death. The dogs in our lives help leaven that understanding, let us rehearse those last breaths.

And, not to be too melancholy, but when I think of my last memory, however many years distant it may come, I imagine that it would be nice to be surrounded by family,

Hank Williams's fine Alabama pining gracing the CD player, and to have my life sealed—as it was opened—by the sweet kiss of a dog. Maybe the gentle lick of a black Lab named Midnight or a miniature poodle named Bijou de Minuit.

Acknowledgments

As much as writers hate to admit it, books are never written in a vacuum. So, a hearty thanks, a wink and a nod to:

Todd Doughty, Phyllis Grann, and Jackie Montalvo at Doubleday, who first saw the potential in this book and then made it happen. And to my agent, Paul Bresnick, for ironing out the wrinkles and tending to the details.

My sons, Drew and Owen, who listened and shared—and, yes, we raised them better than we raised Bijou.

My Friday cronies, Gary Blackman and Herman Gollob, for endless hours of conversation as good and strong as a bitter winter stout.

Toby Bilanow, David Corcoran, and Tara Parker-Pope, friends with keen editorial eyes.

Rabbi Steven Kushner and Cantor Meredith Greenberg and all of my other friends at Temple Ner Tamid in Bloomfield, New Jersey.

Watchung Booksellers and the Montclair Book Center, purveyors of fine books and even finer talk.

Dr. Robert DiPaola and everyone else who helped put me back together at the Cancer Institute of New Jersey.

Dr. Nancy Katz, her canine assistant, Sarge, and the rest of the compassionate crew at Katz 'N' Dogs Animal Hospital in Montclair, New Jersey—they all helped to bring Bijou to this very moment.